STRUCK DOWN
BUT NOT DESTROYED

STRUCK DOWN
BUT NOT DESTROYED

A Mother's Journey through Life's Hardships

DEBBIE DeLINE

TATE PUBLISHING
AND ENTERPRISES, LLC

Published by Tate Publishing & Enterprises, LLC
127 E. Trade Center Terrace | Mustang, Oklahoma 73064 USA
1.888.361.9473 | www.tatepublishing.com

Tate Publishing is committed to excellence in the publishing industry. The company reflects the philosophy established by the founders, based on Psalm 68:11,
"The Lord gave the word and great was the company of those who published it."

Book design copyright © 2011 by Tate Publishing, LLC. All rights reserved.
Cover design by Kristen Verser
Interior design by Stephanie Woloszyn

Published in the United States of America

ISBN: 978-1-61346-658-2
1. Biography & Autobiography / Personal Memoirs
2. Religion / Christian Life / Inspirational
11.10.10

DEDICATION

I dedicate this book to the Lord, Jesus Christ.
I pray He will use it to bring Him glory.

ACKNOWLEDGMENTS

I would like to thank my loving husband, Jon, whose leadership has brought us through many uncertainties. I would also like to thank my son, David James, whose sweet personality is already such a light in an increasingly dark world. You bring such joy to my life, and I'm a better person having known you. I pray that God will give me wisdom to bring out the best in you and that someday you will understand enough to be able to choose to accept Jesus as your Lord and Savior.

I would like to thank my parents, Dave and Ellen DeWitt, who have been tirelessly teaching me God's Word since before I even had a memory and have been invaluable resources during the writing and editing of this book. I want to thank my sister, Becky, who also helped edit the book and has been a godly sounding board for so many situations in my life. I want to thank my sister, Sarah, whose bravery and constant devotion to God and to her family have been such an inspiration to me during my hard times. I want to thank Jon's parents, John and Kathy DeLine, who gave their wonderful son to me and have been an unfailing source of help, encouragement, and love for our entire family. And finally, I want to thank Jon's sisters, Monica and Mikey, as well as all the beautiful women whom God has placed in my life, whose support and friendship have been such a blessing.

TABLE *of* CONTENTS

PREFACE

This book was about seven years in the making, although I only wrote for the last three years or so of that time. A few years before it was completed, I was in Michigan, visiting my family. When I'm there, I like to go out to eat breakfast with my dad, just the two of us. Usually, those family times are so chaotic and our breakfast is really the only time my dad and I get a chance to sit down and talk. At the time, I was really making good progress with my writing, and I was getting some feedback from him. He asked me to summarize the book, so I did, and he said, "It sounds like everything else I've read about suffering." One reason I value my father's feedback is that he doesn't sugarcoat things. And his opinions, while sometimes harsh, are usually correct.

That comment was really meaningful to me, and I've pondered this question several times as a result: "Why am I writing this book?" As it turned out, the question, rather than discouraged me, has only given me urgency to complete the project. It is true that writing some of my most difficult experiences down has been somewhat therapeutic for me. But there are two other more significant reasons why I pressed on to finish. The two reasons come from a passage in God's Word.

In Paul's second letter to the Thessalonians, he wrote, "Having so fond an affection for you, we were well-pleased to impart to you not only the gospel of God but also our own lives, because you had become very dear to us" (2 Thessalonians 2:8).

Throughout this process, I've spoken to a few groups about my son, James, and all the things I've learned from God's Word about dealing with trials. In each case, after I spoke, a small line of women would form to talk to me and share their own trials. Some had cancer, some had sick kids of their own, others didn't know how to help a sick or hurting loved one. They just wanted someone they could talk to who truly understood what they were going through. And they were so hungry for the hope that God's Word could give them about their situation. These women have become dear to me, so this book is for them and others like them.

The format for each chapter is taken from Paul's twofold purpose to the Thessalonians. The first purpose is to share my own life with you. In this regard, this book is totally unique and unlike any other because that is the way God made all of us; our stories, like our fingerprints, are all totally unique. The Bible isn't a book about groups or communities. It is about individuals. In Hebrews 11, the author reviews the story of several individuals from the Old Testament, summarizing by saying, "Therefore [using as an example the race these individuals ran]...let *us* run with endurance the race that is set before *us*..." (Hebrews 12:1, emphasis mine). As you'll see from the pages of this book, my life is very much a work in progress. But I hope my story will encourage you to run with endurance your own specific race that God has set before you.

Hebrews 12:2 goes on to say, "Fixing our eyes on Jesus..." The second purpose of this book is to point you away from this world and all it teaches and instead point you toward Jesus. It is to share not only the gospel of God but to impart to you the hope and love available through the Lord, Jesus Christ. In this purpose, you might find it similar to many other biblically based books or teachings on trials and suffering. At least I hope this to be the case because we all have the same source for our material: the infallible Word of God. I hope in this purpose, with the help of the Holy Spirit, to handle accurately the Word of God and to apply it appropriately to my own situation. And in this purpose, I pray that God would find me faithful.

And in the end, if "my circumstances have turned out for the greater progress of the gospel" (Philippians 1:12), then I am truly most blessed.

FOR MAN IS BORN
FOR TROUBLE

Job 5:7

This is it! I thought. *I'm going to lose him.*

I always wondered if this day might come. I stood there, staring at the pulse-ox monitor that only barely fit on my one-and-a-half-year-old son's finger still hovering in the mid sixties.

He looks awfully gray, I thought.

The men moved around me, almost in slow motion, in the foyer of my house and gathered information, asking me questions. I answered.

Was that my voice? What did I just tell them? I was starting to freeze up. *Call Jon!*

The thought sprung into my head and brought me back into focus. I found my phone on the counter and quickly dialed my husband.

"James has been having a seizure for over twenty minutes now," I told him. "First, he had a ten-minute seizure, and he stopped breathing toward the end. I had to give him CPR. He came out of the first one on his own, but now he's having another one, and he's not coming out of it! I called 911. The ambulance is here now. Yes, he's breathing, but barely. They're giving him oxygen…"

I glanced out the front window. Actually, there were three ambulances and one fire truck parked on the road outside of my house, the lights flashing on all of them. It was just turning dusk, and I watched as my neighbors, one by one, began to emerge from their homes to watch the spectacle.

"I have to go," I said to my husband. "They're going to take him to the hospital."

"I'll meet you there," he said abruptly, and I flipped the phone shut and stuffed it in my pocket.

I watched from the front seat of the large vehicle as a paramedic gingerly carried my son's limp, slightly pulsing body out to the ambulance. My thoughts ran together as I watched.

Still seizing...he has never pulsed like that before...why won't it stop...it always stops on its own...what has it been...at least thirty, maybe forty minutes now...

As the ambulance sped out of our neighborhood, sirens blasting, I prayed urgently to God. *Lord, please don't take him from me! Lord, please help him come out of this seizure! God, please, please, please do not take my little boy!*

"It looks like you have a little boy!"

A tiny burst of adrenaline moved through my body, making my cheeks feel warm. Not that I needed much to feel warm lately, as big as I'd gotten. After trying to conceive for over a year and a half, my husband, Jon, and I were so excited just to have a baby. We always wanted three children, and I didn't so much care about the gender, but I thought he did. I was sure he really wanted a boy, and so I wanted a boy for him. And now, as I lay on the table with the warm goo being pushed around on my belly, I couldn't help but think, *God is so good. He has given us the desire of our heart.*

With a smile, the technician focused in on just the right angle so that it became obvious, even to our untrained eye, that it was indeed very much a boy.

"And what is that right next to...*it*?" I asked.

"That is his hand," she said, and we all laughed.

Lost in the internal revelry of the moment, I was watching the pixilated, black-and-white screen with half interest as the woman proceeded to count fingers and toes. My mind wandered away to tiny blue socks and teddy bears. But I wasn't allowed to remain in this dream for long. It was Jon's voice that brought me back to what turned out to be a much more uncertain reality.

"Is there something wrong with his head? You keep going back to that same area on his head."

By then, I had had enough medical tests to know that the technician is not supposed to give you any information about the outcome. However, sometimes you can get them to tell you when everything looks normal. So when they don't say anything, you feel like you have license to worry. Well, this poor lady—bless her heart—simply told us that she didn't know and that we would have to talk to the doctor. Despite the look on her face, I guess I chose to believe her. Jon did not. Back in the waiting room, he was legitimately concerned.

"It will be fine," I told him. "It's probably nothing." I really believed in my heart the old cliché "These sort of bad things happen to other people, not to me." The discussion with the doctor was brief. She was not any more informative than the technician. The doctor had set up an appointment for us with a specialist the next day to get a more detailed 3-D ultrasound.

I don't remember too much about the one-day wait. I was so convinced in my mind that it would not be an issue that I really didn't worry. But I can say this. Over six years later, I can still remember almost every single detail about the appointment at the specialist: the empty waiting room, the long hallway, the Carolina sweatshirt Jon was wearing, the lime-green decorations in the bathroom, and the feeling of my hopes and dreams of a perfect little boy being crushed into a million pieces.

The specialist confirmed that there was, in fact, something wrong with our baby's head. One of the things that they measure on the ultrasound is the size of the ventricles, the little, sausage-shaped chambers of fluid that run through both sides of the brain. Our baby's ventricles were abnormally large. This condition is called hydrocephalus and is corrected by placing a permanent shunt, or drainage tube, under the skin into the ventricle to drain the fluid. The doctor gave us a short list of potential causes, many of them producing problems in addition to the increased fluid. I think we asked a few questions, but for the most part, we acted like deer in the headlights.

After my second trip to the restroom in just one hour, we were on our way out the door, a little follow-up appointment card pressed into my shaking hand. I was barely able to keep my composure until we reached the elevator. The doors closed. Jon reached out and pulled me in tight as the tears began to come.

I remember so clearly the car ride home. I stared out the window of our navy-blue Subaru Outback, watching the trees and buildings go by in a blur, and thought about how life shouldn't be this way. I couldn't bring myself to look Jon fully in the eyes, fearing I would lose it completely if I did.

"Life is already so hard when there is nothing wrong with you," I told him. "But our poor little guy has problems bigger than mine, and he isn't even out of the womb." I couldn't continue to verbalize my thoughts for fear that I would start crying again, so I continued the conversation in my head. *People get permanent medical conditions in their forties and fifties, maybe in their thirties, not before they are even born. Yesterday, all I wondered about was if the baby would have my dark-brown eyes or Jon's hazels. Will he think out loud like Jon or be quiet and independent like me? Those things seem so silly now. This isn't how life should be, so hard and full of suffering from the very beginning...*

It had already been a difficult two years for us. We moved from our childhood homes in Michigan to North Carolina the summer of our third year of marriage. Jon had only recently recovered from a prolonged illness that had put him in the ER at least once and taken us across the state to various specialists. After a particularly long and dreary Michigan winter, we wanted an adventure and a change of climate, and we got both in Raleigh, North Carolina. We left all of our family and the automotive industry jobs we knew to start a new life, both of us working at a cell phone design company in the up-and-coming Research Triangle Park area near Raleigh.

At first, everything was great. We were learning a new industry, meeting great new friends, and getting involved at a local Bible-teaching church. But by the fall of that year, the layoffs began. Jon's business unit went from thirty-six people down to four. Thankfully, he was one of the four. However, anyone who's been through a layoff can tell you how hard it is when people you've worked alongside and made relationships with lose their job. The man who was in the office next to Jon had been with the company for over twenty-five years.

We were, of course, praising and thanking God that Jon was one of the four who kept his job, but the job went from cushy to pushy in just one day. It wasn't long before he was happy to take a transfer to another business unit. But he was not safe there either. Over the next nine months, there were a series of four different layoffs. If it didn't affect his business unit, then it affected mine.

We were thankful to have kept our jobs so many times, but it was an emotional roller coaster that left us tired and unstable-feeling in our jobs. But by the summer of 2001, the dust had begun to settle, and we were starting to feel safe and secure again—that is until September 11. I think we all learned that day that perhaps there will never fully be the feeling of safe and secure again. I'll never forget standing in the doorway of a conference room, watching the smoke billow out of those buildings, and thinking, *How in the world could someone do such a thing?*

That same summer, Jon was traveling a lot overseas and would leave me home alone for weeks at a time. I was sad to be all alone in this strange city, with no one to call on while he was gone. His travel also didn't help our chances at conceiving. But by the grace of God, by the summer of 2002, I was finally pregnant, and now my baby was sick. What was God doing?

For man is born for trouble, As sparks fly upward.

Job 5:7

I have told you these things, so that in me you may have peace. In this world you will have trouble. But take heart! I have overcome the world.

John 16:33 (NIV)

Do you remember when you were a kid and you didn't have any problems—no worries, no responsibilities?

My sister-in-law asked me this question after an episode with her kids. Her thirteen-year-old daughter called her at work to let her know that when she got home from school, she found water squirting out of some pipes in the garage. By the time she was able to get home, the garage floor was almost completely submerged. She waded through the mess into the house to find her two kids sitting in the living room, eating a snack and watching TV. They were not even the least bit concerned—with the water, that is.

At first glance, the statement seems to be true. But do kids really have fewer problems than adults? For many of us, we tend to focus our memories of early childhood on the good things, like being able to eat a lot of ice cream without gaining weight or doing nothing but playing all day though the summer until we were forced to come in and clean up for dinner.

But upon further scrutiny, I think we'll discover that our trials have been there with us the whole time. We probably can't remember much of our own life when we were two years old, but I don't think I've met anyone with more problems than a toddler. During a visit one summer, my two-year-old nephew cried for an hour when he had to get out of the swimming pool and go home. And you can bet that, while my sister-in-law's thirteen-year-old daughter wasn't going to lose any sleep over the broken pipe, she did have her share of problems to think about. Did she have the right clothes? Do her friends really like her? What about the boy she liked? Perhaps even deeper questions about meaning and destiny plagued her thoughts. In fact, volumes have been written on how to overcome problems we face as teenagers.

The reality is our problems tend to grow up with us. The more mature we become, the tougher our problems seem to get. And the issues that were so important to us when we were less mature tend to fade away as we grow. For example, I was also swimming with my nephew, but I did not cry for an hour when we had to go home, even though I would have preferred to stay a little longer too. In fact, it didn't even occur to me that it might be a problem. As an adult, I've become accustomed to obeying the clock, so I got up and left without hesitation.

As we grow, we gain victory over our struggles. But they never seem to go away. We might have a season where it seems like easy sailing, but at the very best, those seasons tend to end at the most inopportune time with a $500 bill at the car repair shop.

Job was certainly no stranger to trials. He lost his family, his possessions, even his health. In the midst of his sorrow, three friends come to visit him, and one of them, Eliphaz the Temmanite, makes this simple observation: "Man is born for trouble." It's not really a major biblical revelation; it's just a simple observation. If you were sitting in front of a campfire, it wouldn't take much to observe that the sparks fly upward. In the same way, it's not too difficult to conclude that mankind is constantly experiencing trouble from their very birth.

All of mankind experiences trouble. And on top of that, if you are a Christian, you can expect even more trials because of your faith. Jesus reminded His disciples of this fact shortly before He was arrested when He told them, "In this world you will have trouble..."

As followers of Jesus Christ, we have been promised a place in heaven. It is so confident of a reality that Paul talks about it in the present tense as though, in a sense, we are already there, already made citizens (Philippians 3:20). And when we do get to our final destination, we can expect to have a pain-free life (Revelation 21:4). But for a time, we also still live in this world. And while we are here, we will have tribulations. Jesus doesn't say you might run into some issues. He doesn't say that perhaps some of the disciples will have a trial or two. But He makes a confident and all-inclusive statement: "You *will have* trouble."

Jesus seems to be telling the disciples this almost as a word of caution that they should be expecting these trials and that they should be expecting them to be hard. He follows His statement quickly with, "Take heart!" The words could also be translated as, "Take courage!" Why would they need courage if they weren't going to experience difficult trials? You only need courage if you are out in the battle, not if you are at home, in peace and safety.

Realistic expectations are so helpful when dealing with trials. Many times during His life, Jesus told His followers what to expect. In this case, He was saying they should expect to have trouble. Why do we expect a pain-free life? *No one* has one, so why would we think that we should? It is as if we were drafted into the army, went through our basic training, and then we were dropped down onto the beach at Normandy and exclaimed, "Why are they shooting at *me?*" when, in reality, they are shooting at everyone. Why would you expect that some of those bullets would not come your way?

Peter, by the time he wrote his first letter, was no doubt well-acquainted with trials himself and said to the believers he was writing to, "Beloved, do not be surprised at the fiery ordeal among you, which comes upon you for your testing, as though some strange thing were happening to you" (1 Peter 4:12).

Have you ever met anyone who doesn't have a single problem? I have met a few people that, after a casual meeting, I was tempted to assume that. But after getting to know them only a little bit, I've found that there is a skeleton in every closet.

If we're ever tempted to envy someone else's life, if we were honest with our observations, we'd find that we were really only looking at the good parts of their life. We really only wanted that one great thing that they have that has, for all this time, eluded us. And we tend to overlook all the heartaches, pain, and personal discomfort that also come with their life, for no one can escape it.

For those of us who know the Lord, Jesus, there will be a time of peace and safety when we are finally at home with Him. But make no mistake. This world we live in is *not that place*. Rather, this world is a system that promotes selfish desires and "the boastful pride of life" (1 John 2:16). Jesus called Satan the "prince of this world" (John 12:31; 14:30; 16:11), and, like all the things he does, Satan is trying to get you to settle for a cheap imitation of what God has to offer.

God has said of His beloved children that when they get to their final destination, "He will wipe away every tear from their eyes; and there will no longer be any death; there will no longer be any mourning, or crying, or pain..." (Revelation 21:4). So naturally, Satan and his world system are trying to tell you that what God has promised you in heaven you can really enjoy here and now. But God has promised no such thing.

The world encourages you to do everything within your power to promote your own personal safety, security, and a trouble-free life. If you work hard enough and never give up on your dreams, you can achieve this blissful state. The American Dream philosophy tells you that it is completely within your own power to do so. It would have you believe that a stress-free life does exist. Every death is an accident; every sickness could have been prevented with a healthier lifestyle; every difficulty can be overcome by a bit more resources; and every heartache can be covered if you can just find the one with whom you fall madly in love and will, no doubt, make you happy for the rest of your life.

We recently took our son to Disney's Magic Kingdom for the first time. He loved the rides. It was an absolutely beautiful day, and we found ourselves enjoying a funnel cake and an ice cream sandwich in just the right location to catch the 3:00 parade. It had been a magical Disney day. I stood there and smiled with powdered sugar covering just about the entire bottom half of my face as princesses sang and danced, gigantic stuffed dwarfs laughed and jumped, and the kids grinned and clapped to the upbeat music. All the characters were singing, and the words to the song went something like this: "Come and share the exciting adventure of Disney dreams come true…it's time to discover the dream in you…just believe and your dreams will come true (I know mine did), just believe all that you can imagine, just believe and your dreams will come true (they sure will)…just believe and your dreams will come true."

We had a great day, to be sure. And I was actually quite pleased that there were no major incidents or troubles with my son and that the lines were so short. But the joy of that day in no way could compare to the stress and trials of the five years preceding it. And I couldn't help but look at my son and think, *This certainly was not my dream come true. This wasn't what I imagined my first trip to Disney with my own child would be like.*

Please don't get me wrong. I'm not saying that this world is void of joy, peace, or comfort. And I'm not saying that we should avoid seeking good things. We have many happy times in this life, and God has poured out his blessing to us in so many ways. And there is nothing wrong with having dreams and pursuing them fervently.

But we also should expect trouble. And when the trouble comes, we shouldn't run from it or somehow think that it is an accident. Our trials are just as much a part of the way our life is supposed to be as the good times are. It's funny that we never ask, "Why me?" during the good times. Both are essential, and both should be expected. And when those dreams do not come true for you, don't feel as if some great injustice has been done to you. Don't think that you are alone. Don't believe the lie that Disney dreams come true are happening for everyone else but you.

That day, I left the doctor's office thinking, *Why me?* I had lived long enough by then that I should have realized that I was not immune from trials. I should have instead been thinking, *Why not me? What is so special about me that, unlike anyone else, I should escape the tribulations of this world?*

Instead, I thought, *This isn't the way life should be.* I was ignoring what should be plain to any objective observer: in fact, this really is the way life is here on this earth. When we start to accept this reality, then we can move on to how we should deal with these trials. But that day, as we rode home silent in our thoughts, I still had a lot of accepting to do.

I AM FEARFULLY & WONDERFULLY MADE

Psalm 139:14

"Eight."

"That's bigger than last time."

"Yes, a little bit."

I had already had several ultrasounds since Jon and I had first been given the news that our baby had hydrocephalus. We had no further insight into the cause. At every scan, the technician would carefully measure the diameter of the chamber of fluid to see if it was growing normally or if it was getting disproportionately larger.

There really wasn't anything that could be done while our baby was still on the inside. The scans were meant only to know how severe the situation was becoming so the doctors could know what to expect, should the baby decide to come. Still, our mood rose and fell on those numbers as if somehow, if the number was lower, things would be all right.

There was a Boston Market near the doctor's office, and many times after a scan, Jon and I would go there for lunch. Even now, as I think back on that restaurant in particular, it all seems so unreal. After most of our visits, the numbers were worse. So we would usually eat in silence, trying to absorb the reality of the news but never fully being able to. I remember looking around at the other people eating their lunch and thinking, *They have no idea that this terrible thing is happening in our life. They are just having a meal, perhaps observing our silence and wondering, but never could they or would they even care to imagine why.*

Those meals are like a vivid dream to me, the kind that is so real that when you wake up, for an instant, you feel like it was the dream—not your present reality—that is authentic. And you force yourself to go back there and live in the dream just a little while longer, even while, in your mind, you know it was all just a dream. At that point, I was telling myself that it was all a dream. So that is how I remember it.

If you have ever been given a bad diagnosis, then you know that there are usually a multitude of friends and loved ones available with tales of a friend of a friend who was in a similar situation but in the end, everything was all right. We were no exception. And many people had offered us stories similar to ours where there had been some abnormalities on the ultrasound but they worked themselves out by the time the baby was born. There was part of me that really held on to that hope.

But several scans later, the numbers continued to climb. Later that night, I brought my idea up with Jon. James 5:14 says:

> Is anyone among you sick? Then he must call for the elders of the church and they are to pray over him, anointing him with oil in the name of the Lord; and the prayer offered in faith will restore the one who is sick, and the Lord will raise him up...
> The effective prayer of a righteous man can accomplish much.

"You know," I told him, "I've been thinking we should do this."

I wasn't sure how he would respond. Neither one of us was the faith-healer type. But I considered this a command more than an opportunity, and I really felt like we should obey. It wasn't until later that I really studied that passage in James and came to the conclusion that it was probably talking more about a spiritual healing than a physical one. But regardless, it is always a good idea to "let your requests be made known to God" (Philippians 4:6). To my surprise, I discovered that Jon had been thinking along the same lines. That is one thing I love about my husband. I fell in love with him in college, and only after I was too much in love to ever say good-bye did I realize that we think so much alike. He is truly a gift from the Lord. That week, he made the arrangements with the young couples' pastor at our church for the following Sunday.

After the service, we shuffled into the small room just off the worship center designed specifically for prayer. The lights were dim, and it had a cozy feel with couches and leather chairs outlining the room. Several older men followed us in, and it wasn't long before there was a small gathering of the elders of our church. I didn't recognize many of them because we attended a large church. But I felt good about what we were doing.

There were some brief introductions. One gentleman pulled some chairs to the middle of the room and asked us to sit. We explained briefly our situation, the men all put a hand on our shoulders or back, and one by one, they prayed for our little boy and for us. I didn't really expect to feel anything during the experience. But in hindsight, I think that perhaps it was one of the first times in my life that I really felt connected to the body of Christ. These people, total strangers to me, were responding in love to our request, and I felt really at peace.

This is how the church is supposed to act, I thought.

Because we had an ultrasound every week, it wasn't long before we were back at the doctor's office, anxiously anticipating the new numbers. When you go through an experience like we had that Sunday, you can't help but wonder, *Did it work?* We were so happy to hear the news that the ventricle size had not gone up like so many times before and one had even slightly decreased.

We were so relieved and anxious to share the news with everyone who had been so faithfully praying for us. I think there were maybe two or three more scans after that, and each time, the news was good. I was starting to believe that perhaps we had been granted our miracle.

About a week before my due date, we were given a tour of the neonatal care unit of Duke University Hospital, where my son was to be born. It was a private tour, given only to mothers with high-risk pregnancies. It included a tour of the NICU (Neonatal Intensive Care Unit). As I walked through the several large, dimly lit rooms of the unit, looking at all the tiny babies, most of them lying in silence inside clear plastic boxes, being warmed by an overhead light, with little oxygen tubes in their noses, I remember thinking specifically, *We will not be coming here.*

The nurse giving the tour had been given a probable diagnosis by the doctor, and she was tailoring her tour to that. But the diagnosis they had given her was only one of many possibilities that they had suggested to us over the months, and with as many times as they had changed their minds, I just didn't put much faith in it. I was fairly certain at that time that everything was going to be all right. In my mind, the worst case involved a fairly routine shunt surgery when our baby was very young. But that would fix things, and he would go on to lead a healthy, normal life.

I was ten days overdue when Jon and I drove to the hospital. The doctor had finally agreed to induce my labor. Everything was packed nicely in our little suitcase, and we were rushing down the highway because we were late. Our lateness didn't seem to bother the hospital as much as it bothered us, and within an hour, I had had five various tubes and monitors attached to me and was starting to feel the contractions. Because I was being induced, my body oftentimes did not cooperate, and it turned out to be a long labor. Several times, our son's heart rate dropped to unhealthy levels, and at one point, the doctors had me sign a C-section release form just in case it came to that. But during that entire time, I was never worried. I still fully believed that God was going to cause everything to turn out all right.

Twenty-two hours after our late arrival to the hospital, at 6:30 in the morning, David James DeLine came in to the world the old-fashioned way at 8 pounds 12 ounces, with some fine, dark hair and not making a sound. The doctors worked feverishly next to me to try to get him to make some noise. I finally heard one very tempered squeak before they rushed him out of the room and down to the NICU.

I guess it was about an hour before the doctors and nurses were done attending to me and I was able to go visit James. Jon pushed me in a wheelchair past all the other little babies that I had seen only a few weeks before, and we found our little boy sleeping quietly in a little clear plastic box, with a warming light over his head and an oxygen mask near his face.

I learned several days later that the doctors had resuscitated him during that hour. By that evening, he had experienced his first seizure, and they were pumping a narcotic called Phenobarbital into his tiny little veins. It wasn't until late into the night that they were able to take him down for an MRI to see what was going on in his brain.

The next morning, I sat comfortably in my hospital bed, having a lighthearted discussion with my dad. He was happy to have spent the night in a bed back at our house after being up most of the night before with my mom and Jon's parents as they waited out my long labor. I was recapturing all the details of the birth and my run-in with the night nurse in charge of James when Jon entered the room, face red and eyes puffy.

"Dave, can we have a minute alone please?" he asked.

My heart sank when I saw my husband's face. I had never seen him cry. Jon tried to explain what was wrong, but I didn't understand much of what he said. He ended by saying the doctors were waiting to meet with us.

The chief of pediatric neurology, along with a small crowd of medical students and interested pediatricians, had come to James's bedside to talk with us. The head doctor was a tall, thin, older man with crazy gray hair and a bushy, untrimmed beard. He was the only one in the group not wearing a white coat, and I stared at his red flannel shirt that peeked out around the hospital gown that you could tell he rather hastily threw on. He was very straightforward.

"We think your son has a condition called hemimegalencephaly," he said. "It is very rare, maybe a hundred cases in the world. The left side of his brain is two to three times bigger than the right side. The right side is smaller than normal, and the left side has grown around it and is larger than normal. This will give him seizures and significant developmental delays. He probably will never walk or talk. He might need to be fed with a stomach tube. He could have autism. It is really hard to know any definitive prognosis. Every case is different."

"How long will he live?" I asked.

"Oh, it's not fatal. People can die from prolonged seizures, but it's not common. Adults with this type of condition usually die a little earlier than most, say, in their mid sixties, after their parents die and there is no one left to care for them."

Although I don't think I fully absorbed the reality of what he said, it was the first time I remember knowing that James would be living with us for the rest of our lives.

We fired back with several detailed questions about James's future, but in the end, this is what he told us: "This is very rare, and I don't know much about it. I am going to go back and look it up on the Internet. I suggest you do the same, and we'll talk again tomorrow."

Like I said, he was very straightforward, not a characteristic I especially liked at the time but one I would grow to appreciate.

For You formed my inward parts; You wove me in my mother's womb. I will give thanks to You, for I am fearfully and wonderfully made; Wonderful are Your works, And my soul knows it very well. My frame was not hidden from You, when I was made in secret, And skillfully wrought in the depths of the earth; Your eyes have seen my unformed substance; And in Your book were all written the days that were ordained for me, When as yet there was not one of them.

Psalm 139:13-16

I will admit it is hard for me to look at my son and think like David did, that he is "fearfully and wonderfully made." In fact, I'm tempted to say just the opposite. "This one got messed up a bit here, God. You might want to make some revisions on this little guy. He didn't quite come out right."

But then again, was David's body perfect? The Bible does say he was "handsome," with "beautiful eyes" (1 Samuel 16:12), but I get the impression that David was talking about more than just his outward appearance in this Psalm. My son's face is a bit crooked. At first, you might not notice a difference, but if you look at him closely, you will see that his eyes are a bit wider set than they should be. His forehead is bigger on one side than the other, and his left cheek and mouth droop down just a bit. But it is his sandy blond hair and his smile that lights up his whole face that make him an incredibly cute little boy. I know I'm his mom, so of course I'm going to say that. But it isn't because of James's outward appearance that I am tempted to say he falls short of "wonderfully made."

I wonder if David ever had any health concerns. I imagine he did. In fact, at the very least, we all struggle with various types of aches and pains. We all have physical limitations, and there are many days when our bodies aren't cooperating and "wonderfully made" is not the first words we would use to describe ourselves. The human body is marvelous, to be sure, but there are other animals that rival the human body in complexity of form and function. It seems to me that David was hinting at something even more significant.

> Then God said, "Let Us make man in Our image, according to Our likeness"…God created man in His own image, in the image of God He created him; male and female He created them.
>
> Genesis 1:26-27

As humans, we have the distinct honor, from all other created beings, of being made in the image of God. Just like the tabernacle that the Israelites built in the wilderness was made after the pattern of God's holy temple in heaven (Hebrews 8:5), so this tent we call our body, while not having the full glory or full representation, is still in some way built according to the very image of God.

And because we are made in that image, we have intrinsic value. In fact, the God of the Bible is the only One who gives this distinction to mankind. No other religion will hold humans up to this honor.

Even in an increasingly secular society like the one emerging in America, when you strip all religion away, you see a culture where man is only given extrinsic value based on their contribution to the whole. The individual's worth is based on his or her ability to affect the external for the good of society, country, or even immediate family. There is no intrinsic value to the individual, regardless of his or her condition. My son does not have significant value in this type of culture unless *I* place value on him. His value is applied outwardly.

James has recently enjoyed watching the cartoon *Go, Diego, Go*. Diego is an animal rescuer, and during the opening song, you discover why Diego is helping these animals. The song says, "Helping out each other is good for everyone." It implies that the animal he is rescuing is, by itself, not worth rescuing and has no intrinsic value and even the act of helping is, by itself, not valuable. But the fact that helping is good for society as a whole is reason enough to perform the good deed. The value of the animal being rescued is applied extrinsically.

But God has said that all of humankind has value intrinsically. It is not because of anything that we have done or anything we might be capable of doing but simply because we are image bearers—that is, we are made in the image of God. Even our choice to follow Jesus, which does bring us a certain type of glory (2 Corinthians 4:17), is not what gives us value. As Francis Schaeffer put it, "Man is not only wonderful when he is born again as a Christian; he is also wonderful as God made him in His image."[1]

So when Jesus gives the command "Love your neighbor as yourself" (Matthew 22:39), He is doing more than just giving us a way to get along and live peacefully. What He is really saying is, in God's eyes, your neighbor is of equal value to you.[2]

So if we are of such high value in God's eyes, why does He allow the seemingly innocent to suffer? Or, as it is often said, "Why do bad things happen to good people?"

To gain at least some insight into this question, we should again go back to our beginnings. When God created man and woman, they were a perfect creation and existed in perfect relationship with God. There was no sin in the world, no suffering, no sickness or disease. But because of the high value God had given mankind, He gave them a choice. Adam was, to use Francis Schaeffer's term, "an unprogrammed man."[3] He had the ability to *choose* to maintain his relationship with God. God loved Eve and wanted her to *choose* to love Him back. God created a world where it is not truly love when there is no choice.

Of course, God could have created a world where we had the freedom to choose, but we always made the right choice. In fact, the good angels are that sort of creation. Angels clearly have a choice because Satan, along with one third of the angels, chose to rebel against God (Revelation 12:4). But the ones who did not rebel live in a state of perpetually choosing righteously. There is nothing written on why God chose to make our world different from the angels, so we can only speculate. For one thing, we learn more about God's character because of our sinful choices. We would never know about His mercy, grace, or forgiveness if we were like the angels.

God created the tree of the knowledge of good and evil as a way for the man and woman to choose. He would not force them to love Him. He told them that the consequences of that choice were severe. "For in the day that you eat from it you will surely die" (Genesis 2:17). Why so severe? Because the choice was real. If you give me the choice to turn right or turn left but both roads take me to the same place, then is the choice really important? Is it really even a choice at all? If it is truly choice, then the consequences of each choice must be vastly different.[4]

To obey meant life, health, and a relationship with God. To rebel was death, curse, and a broken relationship. We all know how this story ends, as Paul writes, "Therefore, just as through one man sin entered into the world, and death through sin, and so death spread to all men, because all sinned..." (Romans 5:12).

So death entered into the world because of the sinful choice of Adam and Eve. Why do bad things happen to good people? Well, sometimes we find ourselves in a terribly bad situation due to someone else's free choice to sin. A mother loses her son to a drunk driver. A husband has to rebuild his life after his wife leaves him for another man.

But what about the mother dying of cancer, leaving three young children behind? And what about my son, permanently disabled and suffering from a chronic illness before he was even out of the womb?

Paul wrote in Romans 8:22 that "the whole creation groans and suffers." God told Adam, "Cursed is the ground because of you" (Genesis 3:17). Because Adam's choice was real, his guilt was also real. And that guilt had severe consequences—not just for him, but for all of us. One of those consequences is that all of creation has fallen. Mankind once lived in a perfect garden. But because of sin, death entered the world, and every aspect of the world has been corrupted. Not only do humans cause suffering with our sinful choices, but death, sickness, and disease has infiltrated plants, animals, and even humans because of this corruption.

You might be thinking, *But that was Eve. What about me? I didn't eat the fruit.*

Have you ever wanted the one thing you cannot have? Why is it that God can give us so many wonderful things and all we think about is the one thing He is keeping from us? The Bible says that "all have sinned and fall short of the glory of God" (Romans 3:12). Just like Adam and Eve, we stand condemned. We all have rebelled. God has given us a choice, and we have all chosen poorly.

So that's it? One bad choice and we're all condemned and the earth with us? Okay…several bad choices. Still, shouldn't God, out of His great love for us—the love that gave us that free choice to begin with—also provide a way of escape?

That is exactly what He did. Paul said, "For the wages of sin is death, but the free gift of God is eternal life in Christ Jesus our Lord" (Romans 6:23). And just like it was for Adam and Eve, for us, it is all about our choices—actually, one choice in particular. John said, "But as many as received Him, to them He gave the right to become children of God…" (John 1:12).

Do you believe that Jesus was the Son of God? Have you received His free gift of life and forgiveness? It's one simple choice. It's a real choice. Choose Him and you will spend eternity in heaven with Him. Reject Him and you will live forever in your sin and death, separated from God. God will not force you to spend eternity with Him if you don't want to. God loves you enough that He made this choice available to you when He offered His own Son as payment for your sins. "For God so loved the world, that He gave His only begotten Son, that whoever believes in Him shall not perish, but have eternal life" (John 3:16).

Perhaps you've chosen to receive Jesus's gift and He has saved you from your sins but you still don't feel "fearfully and wonderfully made." You understand that after you die, you will go on to live a rewarding life at home with Jesus. But what about the pain we must endure here and now? We eagerly wait for our promised escape that will be waiting for us on the other side of the grave. But how do we make it through *this* life in one piece?

James 1:2 says, "Consider it all joy, my brethren, when you encounter various trials…" How is that possible when at times you are hurting so badly?

The world's answer for this is to just focus on the good, as if somehow there is this great scale, and as long as there are enough good things in your life on one side, it will outweigh the bad on the other side. And if your scale doesn't seem to be tipping, just think a little harder until you come up with some more good things. If you are still lacking, then go after those good things yourself. Work hard and make your dreams come true.

But what if the power of positive thinking just isn't working for you? What if your dream was to have a child and the doctors are telling you it just isn't possible? What if your dream was to get married and you never find that special someone? What if most of the dreams you chase seem to end this way? Or perhaps you have been able to tip that scale and you've found that it still doesn't take away the hurt on the other side. And on top of that, you know that there are some things that weigh so heavily on the bad side of that scale that no amount of good piled on the other side will ever make it tip.

This book is about the journey I've taken over the past six years with the Lord. It is about finding joy in your trials. It's not about tipping the scale or pursuing dreams that might perhaps outweigh your sorrows. And it's not about finding yourself in a terrible rain storm and being able to navigate your way to the quickest cover. It is about standing in the full force of the storm with your feet on the Rock and being able walk away better off than you were before. It is about looking back and saying, "Yes, I was struck down. But I wasn't destroyed. Instead, He lifted me higher."

> I waited patiently for the Lord;
> And He inclined to me and heard my cry.
> He brought me up out of the pit of destruction, out of the miry clay,
> And He set my feet upon a rock making my footsteps firm.
> He put a new song in my mouth, a song of praise to our God;
> Many will see and fear
> And will trust in the Lord.
>
> Psalm 40:1-3

That Rock is Jesus Christ. And if you have not yet chosen Him, then you will find very little comfort in this book. But if He knows you and you know Him, then please come with me on this journey. God is telling a great story in all of our lives. I hope that by sharing my story, your own story will become even more significant, more telling, and sweeter to your soul. "And many will see...and will trust in the Lord."

I AM LIKE A
BROKEN VESSEL

Psalm 31:12

After the discussion with the doctor, we all thought it was best if Jon and the rest of our families spent the night back at our house. Welcoming the privacy, I determined to work at getting my milk to come in. My plan was to breastfeed James exclusively. But there wasn't much about the past few months that had gone according to my plan. After struggling with the breast pump for thirty minutes, I decided to hand-deliver the few drops I'd managed to extract to James's NICU nurse. More significantly, I wanted to say good night to my little guy. We had been together every minute of the past nine months. I didn't like having him so far away. I shuffled down the long, empty halls, trying not to pull a stitch and carrying my jiggling belly in my hands.

Some of the most fragile patients in the whole hospital reside in the neonatal intensive care unit. As a result, it was quite an ordeal to gain access. I gave my name and my child's name to the receptionist, who called back to James's nurse. The nurse approved my visit, and I was buzzed into the washing room, where several large foot-pedal-activated sinks were available. As I scrubbed, I read over, once again, the detailed instructions on how to scrub, how long to rinse, and how much of your arm should be appropriately cleansed. I grabbed a clean hospital gown off the stack behind the sink and put it on over the maternity clothes I rather naively thought I'd be out of by then. Everyone entering the NICU must wear a gown over their shirt to protect the little ones.

I've heard it said that smell is one of the strongest triggers for memory. Even today, six years later, when I take James back to the doctor and happen to use the soap at the Duke University Hospital, I am instantly brought back to the memories of the NICU when James was born.

After delivering my goods, I asked the nurse if she would help me lift James, with all his cords, onto the pillow on my lap. I sat there, looking at his tiny little hand wrapped around my finger when a doctor on the night shift came by to check on him. I thought it was odd that this doctor would be by himself after the crowds we had seen come through there during the day. He completed his examination very gingerly as James lay sleeping on my lap. Even though the lights were all on, it seemed as if I should whisper.

"His nose is crooked," I said to him and ran my finger down James's slightly curved nose.

"Yes," replied the doctor very quietly. He touched James on the forehead, where, if you looked closely, you could also see that something wasn't quite right. He sat there for a minute or two longer. He didn't say anything more; he just gazed at James with a puzzled yet almost amazed expression and then slowly got up and left the room.

I spent the three short days I was allowed to stay in the hospital at the bedside of my little boy. He was hard to hold because of all those tubes and monitors attached to his body. There was an IV in the top of his hand that was strapped with way too much gauze and tape to a soft board that ran the distance from his elbow to his fingertips. There were heart rate monitors, a blood pressure cuff around his calf, a feeding tube down his nose, and an oxygen saturation monitor taped to his big toe.

But usually, with the assistance of the nurse or my mom, who was tirelessly by my side, we were able to lift him from his small plastic box onto a pillow draped across my lap. I spent those days either in this position or in the pumping room as I worked repeatedly to try to get my milk to come in for my baby, who, the doctors told me, might not be able to swallow on his own.

The memories of those three days kind of blend into one, as days often do when they are spent in their entirety inside the lit corridors of a hospital. I hadn't really cried or even had too much time to think. I had a baby to love and take care of, and my motherhood instincts were in high gear. But on the third day, I was given news of what turned out to be the straw that brought me to my breaking point. I was going to have to go home, and my son was not going with me.

All of our extended family had cleared out earlier, and Jon and I were left in silence to pack up our things. We were given a cart, and we rather hesitantly loaded our suitcase, along with the CD player that contained the music I had selected to help with my breathing and relaxation during labor. There were a few cards and gifts, a pillow, and some of Jon's clothes. He had taken a few trips home to pick up some "essentials," so the cart was overflowing with clearly more than we had originally come with.

Soon after we were done loading the cart, a nice young man wearing a blue shirt from transport came with a wheelchair. The three of us rode the elevator down five floors in silence. I kept wondering if the man pushing my wheelchair was curious about where my baby was. If it wasn't plain enough by looking at me that I had just had a baby, then certainly the fact that he picked us up in the maternity section of the hospital would have given it away. Yet my baby was not in my arms.

When we got to the front door, Jon politely informed the man that he was going across the street to the parking garage to get the car. Just as he disappeared out the door, another young man with a blue shirt came to a stop across the hall from us. This man was also pushing a lady in a wheelchair and toting a cart overflowing with bags, pillows, and "It's a Girl" balloons, except this lady had a little bundle of gingerly held pink blankets in her arms.

It was at this point that I totally lost it and began to weep uncontrollably. Jon and I had cried together at the bedside of our son after receiving the news about his condition. But even then it was the controlled, other-people-are-watching type of crying. But now, as I sat there in that chair in the lobby of the hospital, I could not stop the sobs and the flood of tears that streamed down my cheeks and soaked the collar of my shirt. I think at that moment it finally became real for me. Every hope, every dream that I had ever conceived about what it would be like to have a child, was gone.

As the time for the delivery approached, I had been dreaming of what it would be like to bring my baby home. When I purchased the car seat, I had imagined the joy of being wheeled out with him in my arms, tucking him safely into his little seat. It wasn't so much the fact that he wasn't there for this one particular event. It was the realization that none of the events I had ever dreamed about or planned for in my mind would ever come to pass.

The poor man in the blue shirt never made eye contact with me and never said a word—exactly what I needed him to do. At one point, when my sleeves seemed to be completely saturated with tears, he produced—from where, I don't know—one small tissue.

It seemed like an eternity, but by the time Jon arrived with the car, the tissue was way beyond spent. Seeing my face, he moved quickly to load our bags while I climbed into the passenger seat of our car, catching a glimpse of the empty car seat in the back as the tears continued to stream. I cried the entire half-hour drive home.

I am weary with my sighing; Every night I make my bed swim. I dissolve my couch with my tears. My eye has wasted away with grief...

Psalm 6:6a

A close friend called me a few weeks ago, clearly upset. She had given birth to four kids in less than four short years. Her last little boy had been born only weeks before her oldest daughter's fourth birthday. And now her oldest was having trouble sleeping just when she had gotten her baby to start sleeping through the night. She was exhausted. And if that weren't enough, the doctor had recently found several large nodules on her thyroid. She had already battled cancer once as a teenager, and she was scheduled for a biopsy the following Monday.

She was on her way to see her mom for a much-needed break, and she called from the car. After explaining her situation, she was wondering how in the world she was going to be strong through this visit with her mom. She wanted to be a good witness for Christ, but she just wasn't sure how that was going to happen, being so close to the breaking point.

Sometimes it is easier to see things clearly when you are observing other people's lives. It wasn't until that conversation with my friend that I fully realized that relying on our own strength is not what God wants from us. Where does it say that *we* are the ones who are supposed to be strong?

I have another dear friend who suffers from several different chronic medical conditions that cause her significant pain and have also caused her infertility. She loves the Lord and is committed to His Lordship in her life. But she has been hurt and confused many times when other well-intentioned believers have commented to her that she must be a very strong person. "God only gives us what we can handle, so you must be very strong to be able to handle all that," people would say.

The response in her heart has been a logical one: "If this is what I get from God for being strong, then I don't want to be strong anymore."

The Apostle Paul tells us in his second letter to the Corinthians that he suffered from a "thorn in the flesh." There have been many theories throughout the ages about the exact nature of his thorn. But clearly it's not important or Paul would have clarified. What is important to note is that he wanted it gone. The Bible says he *implored* the Lord three times that it might be removed. This word could also be translated as "to beg." Clearly, Paul was fed up with the *thorn*. He was to the point where he was begging the Lord three times for Him to remove it. Certainly, God was able. But He did not remove it.

Why? We don't always know why God chooses to not remove a trial from us. But in Paul's case, God did give an answer. In fact, He gave two. The first answer is, "My grace is sufficient for you..." The second is also helpful: "For power is perfected in weakness" (2 Corinthians 12:9a). Paul had seen a great vision from the Lord, and to help him stay humble, God had given him some weakness. If we want God's power perfected in our lives, it's probably going to involve some weakness on our part.

In other words, it was about God's strength, not Paul's. And "because of the surpassing greatness of the revelations," God had given Paul something "to keep [him] from exalting [himself]" (2 Corinthians 12:7).

This world teaches us that we are the ones who should be strong. If you tune in to Oprah or Dr. Phil, you will hear an encouraging message about how you have all the power you need right inside of yourself to get through your struggle. People wear bracelets that say, "Live Strong." *You* can do it. But what if you can't?

Some people will read this and not know what I mean when I ask, "What if you can't?" But there are others who know exactly what I mean because they've been there. They've been to the very edge of their own strength many times and once or twice were pushed right off the edge. They know what it's like to not handle it.

My friend who has heard that "God will not give you anything you can't handle" is not alone. I've heard from many other friends who have received this news. I myself have heard it. The problem is that it is just not true. I believe the source of it is a misunderstanding of 1 Corinthians 10:13, which says, "No temptation has overtaken you but such as is common to man; and God is faithful, who will not allow you to be tempted beyond what you are able, but with the temptation will provide the way of escape also, so that you will be able to endure it."

Too often, this verse is taken completely out of context. If you read the verses prior to and after this verse, you see Paul is talking about various sinful behaviors. In verse 7, he says, "Do not be idolaters..." In verse 8, "Nor let us act immorally..." The point he is making in verse 13 is that you will not be tempted to sin without a way out. God will never allow you to be put in a situation where you *have* to sin. There will always be a way to choose the righteous thing to do.

Based on the context, it is clear that Paul did not intend for his use of the word *temptation* to mean any general trial or trouble in your life. I suppose if the stressful difficulty, or perhaps sickness, you are facing is causing you to be tempted to sin, then it could apply. God will never give you a trial with which you have no choice but to sin. But He has made *no* promise that you will have the strength to bear all trials or tribulations that come your way. Paul himself told the Corinthians how he and Timothy "were burdened excessively, beyond our strength, so that we despaired even of life..." (2 Corinthians 1:8). That doesn't sound like a guy who was handling it.

In fact, over and over again, Scripture tells us that we should not rely on our strength at all. Psalm 34:18 says God is "close to the brokenhearted and saves those who are crushed in spirit."

Isaiah 40:29 says, "He gives strength to the weary, and to him who lacks might He increases power." So many times we want to jump right to the strength and power part and just skip right over the weary or crushed part. But the two cannot be separated.

King David, a man who experienced many trials, understood this well as he wrote Psalm 31. First, he writes about his position in the Lord: "In You, O LORD, I have taken refuge... You are my rock and my fortress... For You are my strength" (verses 1-5). Then he begins writing about his own condition: "Be gracious to me, O LORD, for I am in distress; My eye is wasted away from grief, my soul and my body also... My strength has failed because of my iniquity... I am forgotten as a dead man, out of mind; I am like a broken vessel..." (verses 6-12).

David describes his condition as "a broken vessel." Are you allowing yourself to be broken before the Lord? In Matthew 11:28, Jesus says, "Come to Me, all who are weary and heavy-laden, and I will give you rest." It is not the ones who are handling their burdens just fine that need rest. It is the weary, the heavy-laden. Do you allow yourself to be weary before Jesus?

David concludes Psalm 31 by saying, "But as for me, I trust in You, O LORD, I say, 'You are my God'... How great is your goodness... Be strong and let your heart take courage, all you who hope in the LORD" (verses 14-24).

There seems to be a process here. First, David acknowledges His position before the Lord. He acknowledges that God alone is his refuge. Then he breaks down in tears before the Lord, admitting his grief, his hardships, his brokenness. I have never come across anywhere in the Bible where it says that it is wrong to have a breakdown. But you can't *stay* broken in your own self-misery. After David wept, he picked up his head and acknowledged that God is trustworthy. And he ended by eagerly expressing his love for the Lord as he is strengthened by *God's* power.

As I talked to my friend about her four small kids and the cancer biopsy coming up, it occurred to me: God never asked us to be strong. He asked us to trust in *His* strength. My friend was going to visit her mom, and she was wondering how she was going to be strong so she could be a good witness.

"Why do you need to be strong?" I asked her. "Cry on your mother's shoulder for a half hour, if you need to. That's what moms are for. But then pick your head up and look her straight in the eye and tell her that you love God and that you trust Him. That is all He wants."

The Apostle Paul had a great response to his thorn:

Most gladly, therefore, I will rather boast about my weaknesses, so that the power of Christ may dwell in me. Therefore I am well content with weaknesses, with insults, with distresses,

with persecutions, with difficulties, for Christ's sake; for when
I am weak, then I am strong.

2 Corinthians 12:10

Even Jesus Himself, being the ultimate example of a godly life, also wept. In John 11, we find the story of Lazarus, a close friend of Jesus. He had been sick while Jesus was out of town, and although his family had gotten word to Jesus to come and heal Lazarus, Jesus had not come. After intentionally waiting for a time, He finally did come. But by the time he arrived, Lazarus had been dead for four days. "When Jesus therefore saw [Lazarus' sister] weeping and the Jews who came with her also weeping, He was deeply moved in spirit and was troubled" (verse 33). And when He saw the place where Lazarus had been buried, the Bible says, "Jesus wept" (verse 34).

Jesus knew that He was going to raise Lazarus from the dead. He had told His disciples He would do it before coming. And He knew that many would believe because of this great miracle. As 100 percent human, Jesus had 100 percent trust in Himself and in the Father to perform this miracle. And yet He still wept. We'll never know exactly why Jesus wept, but clearly it is not a sin to do so.

Romans 12:15 says, "Rejoice with those who rejoice and weep with those who weep."

With every struggle, there is a time for righteous weeping. There is "a time to weep and a time to laugh; a time to mourn and a time to dance" (Ecclesiastes 3:4).

This world wants us to believe that we have the power within ourselves to be strong and handle all our adversity. But sometimes God wants us broken. Sometimes He wants us pushed far beyond any strength of our own. Sometimes He gives us a situation where our *only* response can be to fall on our face before Him, with tears and in great anguish, and to cry out to Him, "Oh Lord, I can't handle this on my own. I can't do this without You."

FOR WE DO NOT WANT YOU TO BE UNAWARE, BRETHREN, OF OUR AFFLICTION

2 Corinthians 1:5

Chug, chug.

Chug, chug.

Chug, chug.

I sat on the couch with half an eye on the TV, listening intently to the monitor, hoping like crazy that James didn't wake up while I was still attached to the machine. I had become accustomed to listening to anything over the steady rhythm of the breast pump that I had hooked to me five times a day. But as any new mother will tell you, it's not something you want to have to stop after having just gotten started.

As it turned out, James spent six long days in the NICU before coming home. And during that time, he passed his swallow study and was doing well with the bottle. I was determined to breast feed, but after two weeks of honest effort, neither James nor I had given any indication that doing it the old-fashioned way was going to be successful, so I was dutifully bound to be hooked to the pump. Being the independent, on-the-go type, it was like torture to be tied down to this machine as it slowly churned out my proof of motherhood, but I was determined to do the best of what was in my control to do to help my baby grow healthy and strong.

I finished and was able to get the parts of the contraption scrubbed clean and the goods safely stored in the FIFO (a manufacturing engineer's term meaning "first in, first out") system I had created in the freezer with fifteen minutes to spare before he woke up. At five and a half weeks old, James was a happy little baby and rarely cried. We played, took a walk with him in the front pack, took turns lying on our fronts and backs, snuggled, and changed diapers all afternoon.

Jon wasn't home. He was on a job-related trip to California. It was the first trip he had taken since James was born. Sleep was a little hard to come by those days, but other than mixing a bit of red liquid medicine in his bottle every morning and night, James came with all the ups and downs that normally accompany a newborn. I seemed to have a handle on taking care of the little guy, and there really hadn't been anything too unusual since we brought him home from the hospital, so it seemed okay for Jon to go. Besides, we were in a tight situation.

Even after his transfer to a different business unit at the company where we worked, Jon never really felt at home in his job. In the fall of 2002, he had decided to enroll in the executive MBA program at the University of North Carolina in Chapel Hill.

We both have mechanical engineering degrees, but I've always been the one who was a true geek at heart. Jon loves business and finance more than physics and mechanics, so he was really enjoying school, even though it was incredibly taxing on his schedule. Instead of becoming tired by the work, the things he was learning only energized him. But still, it wasn't enough. Almost ever since I've known my husband, he has talked about wanting to start his own business. About two months before James was born, he had decided he'd had enough of his big corporate job and he wanted to try it on his own.

That spring, he incorporated as a product development consulting company called Porticos, Inc. The plan was that I would keep my job (and the health benefits that came with it) while he worked to get his company off the ground. And when he had enough business to support our family, then I would quit or work part time and stay home with our son. The trip he was making to California was for a potential business opportunity, and it was critical for him to go.

It was getting to be late afternoon, and optimistically, I thought, *Perhaps I can actually get a shower in before I have to pump again.* I took James upstairs to our bedroom and positioned him carefully in the bouncy seat where I could see him from the shower. I went into the closet to grab some clothes, and when I came out, both of his arms were fixed straight out to the side and he wasn't breathing. I grabbed him up out of the seat and tried desperately to get his attention. He was slightly stiff for another few seconds, but then before I really had time to panic, he was back to normal.

I wasn't sure about what had just happened. I knew he stopped breathing for a time, but it sure didn't look like any of those TV seizures I had seen. After deliberating for a few minutes, I decided to call the pediatrician. To my surprise, they actually seemed quite concerned and suggested I take him to the ER right away.

As it turns out, this would be the first of many trips to the ER for me and James. If I've learned one thing about the ER, it's that if they have you waiting out in the lobby for hours on end, you probably don't need to be there. After telling the triage nurse my story and filling out the appropriate insurance forms, we were quickly led to curtain 4 in the pediatric area.

Apparently ER doctors have a protocol to follow, and when any infant fewer than six weeks old stops breathing, they immediately rule out spinal meningitis. Of course, the only test for that is a lumbar puncture, otherwise dreadfully known as a spinal tap. The doctor suggested that I leave the room.

"Babies usually don't handle these tests well, and parents usually can't handle seeing their baby in that condition," she said.

My heart was breaking, but I decided to take her advice and went outside to get a call off to Jon.

Our conversation went something along the lines of him saying he shouldn't have gone, me saying we had no way to know, and us both wondering if this would be a new way of life for us.

By the time I returned from my phone call, James was sleeping behind his curtain. A nurse was watching after him.

"He did well," she said. "He cried but then afterward fell right asleep, probably from exhaustion…" Her words trailed off as she rested her hand briefly on my back before disappearing to the other side of the curtain.

As it turned out, the rest was brief. Within ten to fifteen minutes, James was up. And this time he was not just tired and cranky—he was hungry. I had left in such a hurry that I didn't have anything to give him to eat except myself. But I hadn't nursed him like *that* for weeks. I tried desperately to get him to eat, but he simply would not. After six or seven failed attempts at latching on, he was crying even louder, and my mid-back muscles were seizing up into tight little knots. The nurse repeatedly poked her head in to observe my failed attempts and ask if there was anything she could do. Feeling so desperately alone and not knowing how to even ask for help, I simply shook my head. Finally, on her third visit (by then I guess the whole ER was getting tired of the screaming baby), it finally occurred to me to ask for a breast pump.

After what seemed to be an hour or two but was perhaps only twenty minutes, she returned with a small hand pump. James had settled down by then, apparently somewhat content with the few drops I managed to get in his mouth. However, content was the furthest thing from describing my personal comfort level. My body was on a schedule, and my chest was telling me that I was about four hours behind. James's failed attempts at eating had only made the situation worse. I no longer felt the muscle pain in my arms or back. I only had one objective, and the nurse had the answer in her hand.

I thanked her quickly and spun around, feverously unbuttoning my shirt when I heard the voice of a young man.

"Ma'am," he said.

My stomach dropped, and I quickly covered myself.

"I'm here to take your son upstairs. We'll be admitting him for the night."

I probably should have just told him to come back, but I didn't. And as a result, I took the longest elevator ride of my life, followed by a grueling walk down a never-ending hallway to the very last door on the right.

Seriously, I was thinking, *the very last room in the hall?*

The polite young man parked my son's bed in the middle of the dark room and left. I didn't even hear the door click, and I was already getting down to business. But I was barely able to get the pump lined up properly to ensure a pain-free extraction when another nurse gave a quick knock and walked right in. Well, I wasn't going to make the same mistake twice.

I looked up at her while holding this clear plastic tube up to my chest and said, "You're welcome to come in, but I *have* to do this now, and I'm not stopping until it's done."

"That's okay," she said rather politely, as if she didn't even see what I was doing. "I just have a few questions to ask."

So I sat there struggling with proper alignment and getting a full stroke on this rather archaic manual pump as she proceeded to ask me for the full, detailed medical history and dietary needs of my son.

Dietary needs? I thought. *Well, that should be an obvious one.*

We stayed in the hospital three days that first time. Jon was out of town. No one ever came to visit. I never asked anyone to come or to help. I wish I would have. I know there would have been several cherished friends who would have quickly been by my side.

Because it took a day or so for the meningitis cultures to grow, as a precautionary measure, the doctors decided to treat James with the full course of antibiotics. And after the negative test and the necessary paperwork, I was carrying my little five-week-old infant down to the car, the strong scent of various drugs emanating from every pore in his body as his little immune system tried to recover from a host of antibiotics that he never really needed.

As I drove home from the hospital, I couldn't help but wonder if this one seizure might only be the beginning.

Blessed be the God and Father of our Lord Jesus Christ, the Father of mercies and God of all comfort, who comforts us in all our affliction so that we will be able to comfort those who are in any affliction with the comfort with which we ourselves are comforted by God.

2 Corinthians 1:3-4

Before my son was born, I enjoyed keeping the details of my life to myself, especially the hard or embarrassing parts. I didn't like sharing my struggles with people, mostly because I didn't want it to be boring for them. We've all, at one time or another, been stuck with that person who just goes on and on about some story, boring us to tears. I didn't want to be that person. And I certainly didn't want to let on that maybe things weren't going all that well for me. I would much rather teach on a great passage or share about something I had learned in a book than give anyone any type of personal drama. And if I did get cornered into sharing a hardship, I tried to downplay it in some type of feeble effort at false humility.

But Paul didn't attempt to downplay his affliction when he was writing to the Corinthians. Instead, he very intentionally shared it: "For we do not want you to be unaware, brethren, of our affliction which came to us in Asia, that we were burdened excessively..." (2 Corinthians 1:8) He gives a couple of reasons why he wanted to share his burdens with them. First, being able to share our hardships is at least one of the reasons why God gives them to us to begin with. Paul says, "But if we are afflicted, it is for your comfort and salvation; or if we are comforted, it is for your comfort..." (2 Corinthians 1:6a). Why did Paul's readers need this comfort? Because they would be, or perhaps already were, experiencing affliction similar to what Paul was experiencing. Being comforted by someone who has gone through a trial similar to yours is a very effective way to patiently endure your own trial (2 Corinthians 1:6).

Another reason that Paul shared his affliction with them was so that they could pray for him. And then when God delivered him from the affliction, many people could be involved in celebrating God's deliverance, bringing more glory to God. "...You also joining in helping us through your prayers, so that thanks may be given by many persons on our behalf for the favor bestowed on us through the prayers of many" (2 Corinthians 2:11).

I have a gentle reminder that I like to give my husband for just about all the people-related issues that he brings home from work: "It's not about you." You would be amazed at how many situations this applies to. It is a good reminder for our trials too. We are tempted to think that during a trial is the one time when we have license to think only of ourselves. But what Paul is essentially saying is, even in the midst of intense suffering, it's not all about you. During our trials, God's comfort comes to us in "abundance." Not just for our benefit, but "...so that we will be able to comfort those who are in any affliction with the comfort with which we ourselves are comforted by God" (2 Corinthians 1:4).

Many times our affliction and our resulting comfort are about others. But ultimately it is all about God. Paul calls God the "Father of mercies," meaning all mercy and compassion originate from God. He is the "God of all comfort." All the comfort you receive and the comfort you give comes from Him. And when you receive comfort, either directly from God or from Him through the life of another believer, it is one more opportunity to respond with a thankful heart and give praise and glory to God.

As James grew and his health issues grew with him, I began to notice that people seemed very interested in his story and mine. And as I began to open up and share some of my own struggles, it gave other people the freedom and the trust to share their struggles with me. Many times we could learn from each other. Sometimes it was just helpful to vent about our day with someone else who understood, and most often than not, we were both comforted by the exchange. It was a big surprise for me to think that my story could actually be helpful to others, that people would even be interested. I was expecting comfort from God, but it was a surprise to me that His comfort came so often through my brothers and sisters in Christ.

God is telling a great story in all our lives. Some of us have some real page-turners. As I've grown through my trials, I've learned to not be afraid to share my life, share my vulnerabilities, be honest with my needs. How are others going to pray, help, or comfort you if they don't even know what's going on in your life? It takes a lot of trust to be vulnerable with someone else. I'm not saying that no one will ever let you down. People are not always trustworthy, so it is a risk. But I do believe that it is a risk worth taking.

NOW FAITH IS THE ASSURANCE OF THINGS HOPED FOR

Hebrews 11:1

Jon's parents were at our house when I brought James home from the hospital. When they returned to Florida after his birth, we had already arranged for them to visit again that week. Jon was also home now, and we were able to have a nice visit. I'm not sure exactly when they decided, but sometime between James's birth and their second visit, his parents had offered to move to North Carolina for a year to help. I have to admit that it was a great surprise to me. And being the strong-willed and independent middle child that I was, it was hard to swallow my pride and admit that I needed help. But pride would be the only reason to say no. There were obviously so many reasons to say yes. If our recent trip to the hospital was not enough, there was one other big thing.

A good friend of mine from work called me shortly after our trip to the hospital. Both of us had been pregnant at the same time, but her baby wasn't due for a few weeks. Calls or visits from our friends were rather awkward at first. It was hard for me because I could perceive their sympathy. And when I saw it in them, I began to feel sorry for myself. I was glad to hear that my friend hadn't called to ask about James. Her news, however, was not good. Once again, all the rumors we'd been hearing about at work were coming true.

Just before I had gone on maternity leave, our business unit had split into two groups, serving two different major customers. And as it turned out, one of those customers was no longer buying. As a result, everyone in that newly formed business unit was going home. Unfortunately, both my friend and I were in that unit. Later that day, the HR representative called to confirm that, along with 250 of my colleagues, I was being laid off.

To be honest, I wasn't extremely discouraged by this. I had picked out a daycare for James before he was born, but it was clear that, given the new information about his medical condition, the place was not a good fit. I was not looking forward to going back to work and leaving my little boy in the care of a stranger. The severance package offered by the company was generous, and it would allow us a few months to figure out what to do.

I guess it was a few weeks later when I got an invitation to lunch from my old boss. He had asked me and two other former coworkers to lunch to discuss an idea he had. He wanted to start a mechanical engineering services business, and he thought the four of us would be a great team. I talked to him and the other guys about some of the work Jon was already doing with his newly formed company, and after significant discussion and review, we all agreed that we would combine the two efforts. In September 2003, Porticos, a product development *and* engineering services company, would officially be five strong. So when Jon's parents offered to come help, I thought this might be just the step up we needed to actually make the thing work.

It was agreed upon that his parents would drive back to Florida to pick up their essentials and then return the following week. My college roommates and I have made it a habit of getting together for a girl's weekend once a year, and it just so happened that our next get-together was in Georgia the very same weekend. So Jon's mom, Kathy, was able to ride with me and James down to my friend's house in Georgia and then continue on with his dad to Florida.

I had a nice visit with my friends, and as the weekend wrapped up, we sat in the airport restaurant, enjoying some lunch before two of them were to return to Michigan. I was watching James nestled in his car seat out of the corner of my eye as I leisurely finished my meal. *There it is again*, I thought. James had been having these strange staring spells, lasting maybe fifteen to twenty seconds. It was so slight that you really had to be looking intently to even notice. He would simply stop all activity and have a blank look on his face for fifteen to twenty seconds and then be back to normal. It had happened once or twice that morning, but as we were sitting there eating, it was becoming more frequent.

I decided to step out of the busy restaurant to phone the pediatric neurologist on-call. After taking him to the ER just a few days before, the last thing I wanted to do was overreact. I explained the episodes as best I could, and in his opinion, what I was describing didn't sound like a seizure, but, of course, I could go ahead and bring him in if I wanted to be sure. With that small chance of hope planted in my mind, I was content to finish my meal and see my friends off. But by the time we left the airport, there was something in my gut that was telling me the doctor was wrong.

I drove the five hours from Georgia back to North Carolina with one eye on the road and one eye on the rearview mirror, where I was able to see James in his seat. Thankfully, he took a good nap during the drive and seemed to be at peace while he was sleeping. But before and after his nap, these episodes went on and even seemed to increase in frequency and intensity. By the time

I reached the vicinity of home, I had decided to drive directly to the hospital.

Jon was able to join us that time, and back behind the curtain in the ER, the neurologist that we had met in the NICU when James was born—the one with the big gray beard and the flannel shirt—had come to observe the events. Even though the physical changes were slight, he was able to see what I was seeing and told me what, by then, I had guessed to be true. These were, in fact, seizures. I thought back over the day and recalled that he had experienced these short seizures maybe fifteen to twenty times that day. The neurologist sat there for twenty minutes to count. James had seven seizures in that time.

They gave him some drugs through his IV, and we waited, but the seizures did not stop. They gave him more, and we waited some more, and finally, he went to sleep, either from the drugs or because it was getting late and he was becoming exhausted from the seizures. The doctor wanted to be sure that his brain wasn't still seizing while he was sleeping, so they ordered an EEG.

By the time the woman arrived with the machine, James was awake and seizing again. The woman took out a tape measure of sorts and began making small markings all over my son's head. She then glued tiny electrical probes on all her markings, maybe as many as twenty probes in all.

Thankfully, he fell back asleep and we were able to confirm that he was not having seizures while he slept. So the answer became rather simple: give him enough drugs to knock him out for a while and hopefully the seizure meds would have had enough time to get into his system and start working by the time he woke up again. So basically, what they did (at least as far as I could tell) was turn his brain off for a time, and once again, we were riding up five floors and walking down that long corridor leading to the pediatric wing of the hospital.

I was so relieved when James woke up the next morning and had stopped seizing. He seemed to be quite hungry, so I prepared his morning bottle. Thankfully, this time, I had all the supplies I needed, having just come from a weekend away from home. James had not eaten much the day before. The seizures had made him lethargic and somewhat uninterested in food. But he was a whole new little guy the next morning, and he gulped his breakfast down in record time.

It wasn't down more than a few minutes, however, before it all came right back up. The nurse and I sat there somewhat stunned for a few minutes with sour milk running down both of our legs and pooling around the base of the chair where the majority of it now resided. She finally ran over to get some towels, and as we cleaned, we were also strategizing and, in no time, came to the conclusion that perhaps James's little belly just wasn't feeling well because of all the medications. I waited several hours and then tried feeding him again. But my second attempt ended quite similar to the first. Thankfully, he had an IV running because, as it turned out, he didn't keep much down all day, and little babies can get dehydrated so fast, especially when they are throwing up as bad as he was.

By that evening, I began to wise up and decided to try only a very small amount of milk: one tablespoon. Even though motherhood comes with no training manuals, the on-the-job training is very effective. There's nothing like being repeatedly sprayed with sour milk to get those wheels upstairs turning. So thinking that, if nothing else, at least this small amount might not get on my shoes this time, I proceeded with caution, and to my surprise, he was able to keep it down.

But boy did it break my heart. He was so hungry. He clearly wanted more than what I gave him, and I wanted so badly to give it to him. Even to this day, there is almost nothing that makes me more upset than to think that my child is hungry. I guess it just seems to me to be my primary responsibility as a parent: to feed my child. And the thought of him going hungry just made me sick.

Thankfully, either that little bit of milk in his belly or the lagging effects of all the medicine was enough to make him sleep pretty well that night. My overly optimistic outlook on life needs but only a little bit of encouragement, so thinking perhaps that a full night's sleep had improved the situation, I decided to give him three tablespoons of milk for breakfast the next morning.

As I cleaned James's breakfast off my shoes, I still couldn't help but think that all he needed was a bit more time to get the medicines out of his system and he'd be okay. I waited another few hours and went back to the one tablespoon amount, and he was able to keep it down. As the day went on, I found that I could shorten the wait time between feedings with some success. But if I tried to give him more than one tablespoon, it would all just come right back up. It wasn't an ideal situation to leave the hospital with, but Jon and I figured that as long as he was keeping something down, it was safe to take James home. So we went about doing all we could to get out of there as quickly as they would let us.

James was already taking one anti-seizure medication, but the doctor had decided to send us home with another. This new medicine was not really made for kids yet. It came in a capsule with hundreds of small beads inside. I was supposed to break open the capsule and mix the beads in with his milk so that he would drink them down. I, of course, assured him that it would not be a problem, having really no assurance myself but knowing how urgently I wanted to get James home.

By the time we were all home, Jon's parents were back from Florida. I don't know how I could have gotten through the days that followed without Kathy there to help. We were a good match because she is an early riser and I don't mind staying up late. For the first two days, we adhered strictly to the one-tablespoon rule and fed James this quantity about every thirty to forty minutes around the clock. We would sort of take turns during the afternoon and evening, but Kathy would go to bed early. I would stay up until James went to bed and then set my alarm to go off every half hour. I would get up and give him the one tablespoon of milk and then go back to sleep for one half hour and then up again. At about 5:00 a.m., Kathy would wake up and take over for me until about 10:00 or 11:00 so I could get a solid five or six hours of sleep.

For the first few days, this seemed to work well, but by the third day, James didn't want anything to do with eating at all. He had lost his appetite completely. Now we weren't so much worried about him throwing up the milk. We couldn't even get him to swallow it. It had been five or six days since he had anything substantial to eat or drink, and I was beginning to get really worried about dehydration, as well as just overall calorie intake.

Instead of giving him his bottle, we switched to the oral syringe so we could squirt the milk directly into his mouth 1 mL at a time. Sometimes he would swallow it on his own, but most of the time, we would have to trick him into swallowing it by putting his passy in his mouth or trying to massage his jaw and throat. We continued with these methods, one teaspoon at a time, every half hour throughout the day. During the night, I found that he would eat from the bottle better because he was actually sleeping through it and just sucking and swallowing from a reflex more than anything else. That is when I found it easiest to get those little beads down him. Of course, I wasn't getting much sleep, but poor Jon wasn't either. And with his parents in our guest room, there wasn't anywhere for him to go.

We kept this routine up for a full week at home before I decided to call the neurologist to find out if he had any suggestions. If I had read the small print on the prescription paper for those little beads, I would have known that the medicine is also used sometimes as a diet pill, as loss of appetite was one of the major side effects. No one had told me to look for that, and, of course, I didn't read the small print, so it never occurred to me that the beads might be causing the issue. I had it in my head that the loss of appetite was somehow related to the upset stomach he had in the hospital, and why would you call a neurologist to help you with an upset stomach?

The doctor decided to switch James to a different seizure medication. The hope that we had found the answer was just enough to give us the strength we needed to continue the around-the-clock feedings. We did this for another seven days before we saw any signs of James' appetite returning. It was another two weeks before he transitioned back to a more normal eating schedule. He had lost about one pound; 7 percent of his body weight.

Consider it all joy, my brethren, when you encounter various trials, knowing that the testing of your faith produces endurance.

James 1:2-3

The word *trial* used here in James is the Greek word transliterated as "Peirasmos," and it means "an experiment" or "the trial of one's fidelity, integrity, virtue, or constancy."[5] The author of James is saying that if you find yourself in a trial, know that it is a test of your faith. And we should consider it joy when our faith is put to the test because it gives us the opportunity to give legitimacy to our faith and build endurance or maturity.

Adding legitimacy to your faith can be a great testimony to those around you who are watching. My dad loves the Word of God, and he also loves airplanes. And as a result, many of the illustrations he uses when teaching the Bible somehow involve airplanes. When writing a commentary on the book of James, he gave the following illustration:

> You've been invited to fly around the world in an airplane. There are two possible airplanes you can choose from. Both are new, but one has been taken up by the test pilot, been put through maneuvers, and everything that could go wrong has been tested, it does well under turbulent air, and it works fine. The other airplane has just rolled off the assembly line. It should be just as good as the other one, but it's never been tested. Which airplane would you rather fly around the world in?[6]

We've already learned that everyone living in this fallen world has trials. If someone who was not yet a follower of Jesus was carefully observing two different friends and one had come thorough many difficult trials and was able to still stand strong in her faith, while the other friend never seemed to have any significant problems at all, which one do you think she would be more likely to be drawn to when faced with her own trials? Which one to you think she would go to for love and support when she so desperately needed a friend?

James says we are to "consider it all joy" in our trials, not just because they give an opportunity to build legitimacy, but trials also allow us to exercise our faith and, by exercising it, build endurance. Let's say that your desire was to run a marathon.

In your mind, you really believed you could do it. You made a decision to participate and mailed in your entry form, thinking that when the time came for the race, you knew you would be ready. But then in the three months leading up to the race, you never went out and ran even a single mile. How do you think you would do come race day? If it were me, I would have a hard time making it to mile five without losing my cookies.

As a follower of Jesus, our walk is a walk of faith: "For we walk by faith, not by sight" (2 Corinthians 5:7). And if we want the endurance James writes about, our faith must be exercised. Our muscles become more consistent with use. Our minds are sharpened with use. Our love is more steadfast when we take the chance to show love. Why would it be any different for our faith?

Trials give us the opportunity to exercise the faith we already have. They don't necessarily add new faith. Only revelation from God's Word can add new faith. "Faith comes from hearing, and hearing by the word of Christ…" (Romans 10:17). For example, how are we to have faith that God loves us unconditionally if we had neither read in God's Word nor had anyone ever revealed to us that He does, in fact, love us unconditionally? So new faith only comes from believing in revelation that is new to us.

Sometimes trials have a negative effect on people. What if someone goes through a trial that we thought would have helped that person gain endurance in the area of God's unconditional love for them but the person actually never heard that God loved them unconditionally, or maybe they had heard it but never truly believed that about God? In this case, the trial could actually have the opposite effect of what we were expecting. The trial could serve to push them away from God because the original faith was never there.

But once we have learned something specific about God and have chosen to have faith in it, then that specific faith that already exists in us can be tested and given more endurance through trials. If I had no leg muscles, I could never run in a marathon. But because my leg muscles exist and I am using them today, after I exercise them, they have more endurance.

The author of Hebrews tells us, "Now faith is the assurance of things hoped for, the conviction of things not seen" (Hebrews 11:1). When you are hoping for something, it means that you have not already obtained it.

And just to make it abundantly clear, the author of Hebrews follows by saying that faith is not just the assurance of things hoped for but it is "the conviction of things not seen." Paul writes in Romans 8, "For in hope we have been saved, but hope that is seen is not hope; for who hopes for what he already sees? But if we hope for what we do not see, with perseverance we wait eagerly for it" (Romans 8:24-25). So not seen means, well, *not seen*. It might sound silly, but the point I'm trying to make is that if you are going through a trial where your faith in God's love for you is being tested, you're going to have to go through a time when you really don't *see* His love for you at that moment. If you want to become more steadfast in your faith in the truth that God will never desert you or forsake you (Hebrews 13:5), you're going to have to go through a time where He seems distant or absent from your life. Faith is the assurance of things *not seen, not felt, not experienced, not fully understood.*

Earlier in His ministry, Jesus addressed this issue of faith with His disciples. Several of them were on a boat on the Sea of Galilee when a great storm rolled in and the waves were covering the boat. Where was Jesus during this scary and difficult time? Sleeping. Do you ever feel like Jesus is sleeping through your storm? Finally, being truly concerned for their own survival, the disciples woke Jesus up, saying, "'Save us Lord; we are perishing!' He said to them, 'Why are you afraid, you men of little faith?' Then He got up and rebuked the winds and the sea, and it became perfectly calm" (Matthew 8:25-26).

It is worth observing that Jesus's first response is not to fix their problem. His first response is to ask, "Why are you afraid?" And then, only after observing how small their faith was, He took away their trial. You see, once God takes away our trial, our opportunity to prove our faith is over. When faith becomes sight, it is no longer faith.

Thankfully, many of our faith-testing experiences do end rather climatically in sight. God gives us plenty of opportunities to see Him in our lives. And when we do get those small glimpses here in this world, it encourages us all the more to have faith in God for the many things that will not become sight until we get to heaven.

I love those mountaintop times that God gives us when He seems so close and I am able to breathe easy, resting securely in His arms. But it usually isn't long before He's got me back in the boat and a storm is on the horizon. When I was a new believer, there were many long and drawn-out opportunities for sight. But as I grow closer to God, I find that I am able to endure longer and more strenuous times of faith. I am building endurance.

Before Jesus was arrested, He told Peter, "Simon, Simon, behold, Satan has demanded permission to sift you like wheat; but I have prayed for you, that your faith may not fail..." (Luke 22:31-32a). Jesus wanted what was best for Peter. And perhaps knowing what Peter would have to endure later in life, Jesus permitted Satan to bring about trials in his life. Isn't it great to think that Jesus is praying for you during your trial? He is our Advocate before the Father (1 John 2:1; Job 16:19). He is our greatest supporter.

One big question in this faith exercise still remains. If faith is "the assurance of things hoped for," then what specifically should we be hoping for? What specifically should we be trusting in that is "not seen"? Some people make the mistake of thinking that God will give us exactly what *we* want if we simply have enough faith. It is true that Jesus did promise this type of response to some specific people for a specific time period while He was here on earth (John 14:13-14). And it might turn out to be your experience that God does calm your specific storm. But He never made that type of general promise that applies to you and me for all our situations. In fact, it doesn't even make sense to think that somehow we could control the God of the universe and get Him to do whatever we want Him to do simply by turning our faith up high enough. God might choose to answer our prayers according to our liking and give us many good things. I'm not talking about that. What I'm saying is that we cannot force His hand or somehow coerce Him, even with our faith.

We cannot force God to do what we want. But be sure that we can trust Him to be completely faithful when He makes us promises that are in accordance with what *He* wants. Like Abraham's wife, Sarah, who "considered Him faithful who had promised" (Hebrews 11:11). God will always keep His Word. And by His grace, God has given us many specific promises that apply to us during our time. These promises are what we should be hoping for. These promises, while sometimes not seen, are what we should trust in.

Hebrews 11 gives us a long list of people in the Old Testament who acted bravely in faith, trusting in God's promises. One of those on the list is Abraham. God had promised Abraham that his descendants, specifically through his son, Isaac (Genesis 21:12), would be numerous, like the stars in the heavens (Genesis 15:5). And through a specific descendant of Isaac, all the families of the earth would be blessed (Genesis 12:3). But then, of all things, God asked Abraham to kill Isaac as a sacrifice.

> By faith Abraham, when he was tested, offered up Isaac, and he who had received the promises was offering up his only begotten son; it was he to whom it was said, "In Isaac your descendants shall be called." He considered that God is able to raise people even from the dead, from which he also received him back as a type.
>
> Hebrews 11:17-18

Abraham was so sure that God would keep His promise of giving him descendants through Isaac that he actually tied his son up and was going to kill him, figuring God would just raise him up from the dead (Hebrews 11:19). Who could be strong enough to sacrifice their own son? Only one who knew that he would not be dead for long. Abraham believed that God would keep His promise. What actually happened was that God stopped Abraham's hand just before he killed Isaac and He Himself provided a substitute sacrifice.

Paul also spoke of Abraham's faith in Romans when he said of him, "Yet with respect to the promises of God, he did not waver in unbelief but grew strong in faith, giving glory to God, and *being fully assured that what God had promised, He was able also to perform*" (Romans 4:20-21, emphasis mine).

Are you aware of God's promises to you? Are you absolutely convinced that if God said it, He is certainly capable of performing it? Are you so sure that you would even trust God with the life of your child?

There are many promises to us in God's Word that we can rest in. In the next few chapters, I want to study a few of those promises, hopefully adding some new faith for some or reminders for others. I've picked the ones that have meant the most to me. These are the promises that I have hoped in through my toughest storms. Some I trusted from the beginning and have grown in my endurance. Others forced me into God's Word for answers, and I was able to grow in faith as a result. And I continue to struggle with some today. I have not even come close to understanding the depths of them all. But I hope that you can come to understand them just a little bit too and stand firmly on their truths as you weather even the toughest of your storms.

Some of God's Promises to His Followers

God is in control of the world and everything in it.

God loves you.

God has a plan. Everything has a purpose.

God is working everything together for the greatest good to those who love Him.

We can trust Him.

God is preparing a place in heaven for those who accept Him. And someday, His children will live there forever with Him. And when we get there, He will reward us for our faith here.

I don't think I read my Bible once during the whole first three months of James's life. If I prayed, it was perhaps an urgent, pleading two-minute prayer at best. Before he was born, I had made it a habit of reading my Bible before bed. I started this ritual when I was in the eleventh grade. I began reading in Genesis, and it took me seven years to get through the entire Bible. Needless to say, ritual is a gross overstatement, as there were several nights that the reading got skipped, especially during those college years. But the next time around, I finished in only four years. I certainly wasn't setting any records, but I never gave it up. That is, until my son was born. All those years, I read out of obedience and occasionally out of interest or pleasure. But when the time came that I needed that information the most and had no time to stop and read, it was already there in my head.

One day in the hospital that second time, the nurse came in our room, and as she was adjusting James's IV, she said that she had been talking with the other nurses about how calm I was and how well I seemed to be handling all that was happening. I hadn't even realized it until she said it that I *was* calm. I asked her if she had ever read the "Footprints" poem. I use to make fun of that poem because it was so widely circulated when I was a kid. It was on every shirt, cup, pen, poster, card, box, or trinket in the Christian bookstore. Looking back, I know that I laughed at it because at that point I had never experienced a need to be carried by God. But I told the nurse that day that I belonged to God and it was Jesus who was carrying me. He was giving me the peace that she saw.

Footprints

One night I dreamed I was walking along the beach with the Lord. Many scenes from my life flashed across the sky.

In each scene I noticed footprints in the sand. Sometimes there were two sets of footprints, other times there was one only.

This bothered me because I noticed that during the low periods of my life, when I was suffering from anguish, sorrow or defeat, I could see only one set of footprints, so I said to the Lord,

"You promised me Lord, that if I followed you, you would walk with me always. But I have noticed that during the most trying periods of my life there has only been one set of footprints in the sand. Why, when I needed you most, have you not been there for me?"

The Lord replied, "The years when you have seen only one set of footprints, my child, is when I carried you."[7]

We need to understand God's promises in the easy times. Usually it is hard to pull out your Bible, read, or even pray during the storm. During this particular storm, I barely had time to eat and sleep. If you are constantly building your knowledge of God, you will have some solid truths to believe in when the storm comes.

During the first year or so of James's life, looking back, I see that God carried me a lot. But as time went on, it seemed as if He was less likely to show up with that "peace…that surpasses all understanding" (Philippians 4:7 NKJV). At some point, I needed to be able to trust Him when no peace was to be found. He was building endurance in me.

IN HIM, WE LIVE AND MOVE AND EXIST

Acts 17:28

The five owners sat in the conference room of our empty office, no one really looking at each other, but instead, everyone stared at the floor or table or anxiously fiddled with their pen. We had all talked about it with each other one-on-one, but now we were getting together to make it official. Despite our best efforts, we simply didn't have enough paying customers in our company, now one and a half years old, to support five people's salaries. Two of us would have to step aside. The other four decided that they would wait one more week for someone else to voluntarily leave or there would be a vote.

I was really at peace with the decision for me to stay home. After Jon's parents had gone back to Florida over two months before, I had been driving James to a developmental daycare about thirty minutes from the office. On paper, the place seemed to be all that he needed. No other daycare seemed anxious to take him, given his condition, and this place was especially designed for children with disabilities. But in reality, it was a terrible mess. The place was dirty, the staff was sketchy at best, turnover was frequent, even the food seemed tasteless. In addition, James's seizure activity seemed to be increasing, and I was anxious to have him at home where I could devote all of my attention to his care and development. Besides, not being a true entrepreneur at heart, I had grown tired of the endless cold calls and ambiguity of self-driven projects.

Later that week, I met privately with my former boss who had originally come to me with the idea to start his own company. Clearly, he had a passion and a determination to make this work based on his initiative and past performance. I sat down with him to make a plea on Jon's behalf for the same reasons. After all, Jon had been the one who started Porticos. It was his baby. He had wanted to be a business owner as long as I had known him. He had stepped out on his own initiative while the other two had simply been conveniently available due to the layoff.

Being a kindhearted and patient man, we had a good discussion, and I felt pretty certain that Jon would remain in his current position. The wife of one of the other guys was employed full time with medical benefits, so he seemed the most logical to go, given the extra financial security he had over the rest of them.

But my conversations with Jon were not so certain. When we first lost our medical insurance after I was laid off, we applied for Medicaid for James. Medicaid is a government-funded health care program. Qualifying for it is almost entirely based on a person's household income. At the time, we had no income, so we easily qualified. But we had to re-qualify every year, and now, a year later, as two-fifths owners of our company, our household income was considered to be two-fifths of the business' income for the year, no matter if we actually took that money as salary or not. But as I mentioned, times were slow, so the net amount wasn't very much, and we qualified for a modified state-sponsored program where we had to pay a monthly premium for James, but it was reasonable.

Jon and I had been buying our own health insurance at a reasonable rate, and when we received a quote for James from the private insurance company, given his pre-existing condition, we were quoted a premium of about $700 per month just for James. We were paying just under $200 for bare-bones coverage for both of us. So if we paid these premiums, together, we would be paying just about the same amount each month for health care as we were paying for our mortgage. And that was just the premiums.

We couldn't decide what to do. We were okay for the next year, given the state-run program, but if we were successful at all with the business, there was no way we would qualify the following year. Jon was really on the fence about what to do. I felt sure that one of the other guys had it in his mind to step aside if no one else did. So it really was up to Jon if he wanted to stay.

I couldn't imagine walking away from all that we had built over the last year and a half: so many pleading sales calls, so many days without pay, so many days working all day and through the night to meet customer deadlines. And where would he get a job if he left? I certainly didn't want to move to another city. It had taken a long time to get connected, but we had finally joined a small group Bible study near our house with some great couples. The women in the group recently started getting together for a Bible study once a month, and I had rather eagerly volunteered to lead it. I enjoyed our church. I didn't want to find new doctors and therapists for James. Really, the list of reasons to not leave town could have gone on and on.

I also knew that Porticos wasn't all that Jon had dreamed it would be when he started it. The type of work we were getting wasn't the type of work that he particularly enjoyed. It was more suited to the other guys. There were no hard feelings between Jon and them, but they had taken a little bit of a different direction than he wanted to go. Not that it was directly opposite; it was only slightly different. We were aware of some of the differences going in, but it was hardly noticeable at first. However, as time went on, it was clear that one was always tugging at the other, and like two animals yoked together and wanting to walk in slightly different directions, one was always being pulled slightly off course by the other. You can't walk long in that condition without beginning to feel fatigued by it. But at the same time, no two people are alike. Won't there always be these types of tensions in any team you form?

The morning of the vote came, and Jon still had not decided. Jon and I went out to lunch together that day and discussed it one last time. We covered all the details of the type of work that the company was getting, what Jon's ultimate goals for his career were, how much work we had already invested, if partnering with these men was what he wanted long term, and if we would be able to care for James properly and give him the therapies and possible surgeries he needed. The conversation over lunch ended the same way all the others had. He just didn't know.

We went back to the office, and one of the guys poked his head into my office and said, "Well?"

"I don't know *what* he is going to do," I said, wondering if he believed me because I couldn't quite believe it myself. My husband is always planning at least six months into the future. I couldn't believe that he was keeping us hanging like this up until the very last minute. It just wasn't like him. But then that is what made me all the more convinced that this was going to be an incredibly hard decision for him to make, no matter what he chose.

I watched the ten slow minutes before the meeting click off one by one in the bottom corner of my computer as I busied myself with nothing important. I grabbed my cell phone and was getting up to head down to the conference room when Jon showed up at my office door. I met him in the doorway, and as we walked together down the hall to the meeting, he leaned over and whispered in my ear, "I'm out."

Four weeks later, all of our earthly possessions were packed in boxes, and we were moving to a city called Greensboro, eighty miles west of Raleigh. I just couldn't believe that we had to move and start over again, finding new friends, a new church, new doctors, and a new home. But mostly, I couldn't believe that we were walking away from the company that I thought was going to be our future. By that time, I was growing accustomed to not reacting emotionally to the dramatic ups and downs of our life. Not because I had grown into some type of super saint; I just couldn't do it anymore. At some point, you just can't cry anymore about the small things or even the medium things. My son was alive and doing okay. My husband and I were surviving. And Jon now had a good-paying job with good medical benefits. I had to rest knowing that God was in control. He had appointed the boundaries of our habitation, and obviously, those boundaries included Greensboro, North Carolina.

The God who made the world and all things in it, since He is Lord of heaven and earth, does not dwell in temples made with hands; nor is He served by human hands, as though He needed anything, since He Himself gives to all people life and breath and all things; and He made from one man every nation of mankind to live on all the face of the earth, having determined their appointed times and the boundaries of their habitation, that they would seek God, if perhaps they might grope for

Him and find Him, though He is not far from each one of us;
for in Him we live and move and exist…

Acts 17:24-28

God is intimately involved in all aspects of your life, especially your trials. He has determined the exact time that you will be born and when you will die. He has determined the exact places you will live. He has even numbered the hairs on your head (Matthew 10:30). In fact, all of the details of your life have been carefully orchestrated to help you find Him. God eagerly desires a relationship with you, and He has designed your life's situations so that you would reach out to Him. He is never far.

While God is sovereign and in control of every detail, it is also clear that He has set up nature to be governed and controlled by a set of physical laws. God might choose to overcome those physical laws for His own purpose, as in the many times Jesus healed sickness while on earth. But we shouldn't act recklessly, assuming He will do this every time. He has told us that we can expect to live with the natural consequences of our free-will choices (Galatians 6:7).

For example, you shouldn't cross the street without looking both ways, reasoning that God is in control of whether you get hit by a car or not. Our job is to look both ways. God's job is to decide if we get hit by a car or not. So often we get caught up trying to control God's job while neglecting to do our own. As a result, we end up stressed over things we cannot control while making poor decisions about the things we can.

Many of our trials fall into the category of things we can't control. Our human nature wants to control everything, so this lack of control can make us feel anxious and dismayed. But God is never out of control. Not only does God know every detail of what you are going through, but He also loves you with an unfailing love.

> Who will separate us from the love of Christ? Will tribulation, or distress, or persecution, or famine, or nakedness, or peril, or sword…But in all these things we overwhelmingly conquer through Him who loved us. For I am convinced that neither death, no life, no angles, nor principalities, nor things present, nor things to come, nor powers, nor height, nor depth, nor any other created thing, will be able to separate us from the love of God, which is in Christ Jesus our Lord.
>
> Romans 8:35, 37-39

Probably the most important promise in all of Scripture is the promise of God's love for us. In Romans 8, Paul lists several things that might tempt us to think that God doesn't love us: distress, persecution, peril. While these things can sometimes cause *our* love of God to fail, nothing at all—not a single created thing—will cause His love for us to fail.

Are you absolutely convinced of God's love for you like Paul was? Has a trial led you to conclude that perhaps God doesn't love you? Nothing could be more wrong. In fact, it was out of God's great love for us that He sent Jesus to die for our sins. John 3:16 says that "For God so loved the [people of the] world, that He gave His only begotten Son…"

God loves us, and He knows exactly what we are going through. He knows every detail, how it is making us feel, how hard it is to endure. He knows.

David said to the Lord, "You have taken account of my wanderings; Put my tears in Your bottle. Are they not in Your book?" (Psalm 56:8). God knows that you are hurting. He has taken it into account. Not one tear has been shed that He has not kept track of.

God knows, God loves you, and God is in control.

THE LORD HAS MADE EVERYTHING FOR ITS OWN PURPOSE

Proverbs 16:4

I sat up rather quickly, grasping for the metal bowl down by my knees and, for the third time in the past two hours, emptied my entire stomach contents into the bowl. Of course, there wasn't much left at that point and, based on the amount of time I had also spent on the toilet in those two hours, I was willing to bet that my entire GI tract was completely empty by now.

Jon sat across the room on the love seat that came with our temporary furnished corporate apartment in which we were living in Greensboro. The place was decent, but all the furniture was well-used, including the couch that I had covered with sheets and was now throwing up on. I wondered how many others had done similarly disgusting things on the couch or on the beds before we got there. It didn't take long for my mind to drift to possibilities even worse as I looked down at James, now a year and a half old, playing on the stained carpet.

Jon got up and took my bowl to empty it, and I laid back down, too weak to sit up for long. I knew this was a temporary bug because poor James had been throwing up only a few days before. Like any sickness for him, it had been accompanied by many seizures, but he had started to get better only the day before, and as I felt incredibly miserable, he seemed to be completely recovered.

Jon had already been working in his new job for two months and seemed to really enjoy it, but the hours were long. He worked every day until about 7:00, when he would come home for dinner and spend some time with James.

I had been spending my days looking at houses. We wanted a single-story house because we were pretty certain that James wouldn't be walking soon. He wasn't getting any smaller, and the thought of carrying him up and down a flight of stairs two or three times a day seemed impractical. Plus, he might someday be able to get around in a walker with wheels, so we were looking for a house that didn't have any stairs and had all wood floors. We finally found a great house that was half built out in the country, about a fifteen- to twenty-minute drive from Jon's work. We were only planning to be in the corporate apartment for three months, but with the house not completely finished, that three months turned into four.

James's illness and now mine had taken away from the valuable four weeks remaining in which time we were to finish picking out tile, carpet, paint colors, light fixtures, cabinets, knobs, etc. I couldn't believe how many decisions there were to make. And we didn't even start from the beginning. But it was fun to take on a decorator role, and I really did love the new house. We were living in a townhouse in Raleigh while Jon finished up school, and it never really felt like home. Although only partially finished, I could already tell that this new place was going to fit our family just right.

This illness was also setting me back in my exercises with James. In the past six months, James had started weight bearing on his legs, and by the time we moved into the apartment, he was actually standing with his full weight on both legs. He required maximum assistance for balance, but he was fully supporting himself. However, he had no concept of taking steps. Using the move as an opportunity for a fresh start with some new goals, I had been trying to teach him how to take steps. I don't know why, but he seemed to be completely missing that instinct. Most kids at that age, when you lean them forward, will at some point instinctively put their foot out in front of them. But I could bend James down all the way to a 45-degree angle or more and those little feet would not budge. It was as if they were bolted to the floor.

It was the middle of winter, I didn't know a soul in town, and there wasn't much house to keep inside the small apartment. So I would spend my days hunched down on all fours, with James's arm around my neck as I slowly grabbed each leg by the ankle and moved it forward, one step at a time. We went back and forth across the living room in the apartment three or four times a day. It would take twenty to thirty minutes to do just one lap because he was not cooperating at all. He wasn't working against me necessarily, but he absolutely didn't get the concept. I had made a commitment to do these exercises daily, but as the new house tasks were ramping up, it was becoming harder to squeeze in, and this illness had brought it to a temporary halt. It has always been frustrating for me to make plans and then fail to keep them, even if the circumstances were beyond my control.

I recovered quickly enough, but as soon as I felt better, another problem started to emerge that would take me even further from my goals. I had been feeding James rice mixed with formula for months, and he seemed to do well with it, so three months prior to moving, he transitioned to baby food with no issues. But he couldn't get the concept of chewing, so finger foods were not an option. Mostly, he would just spit the food out, but sometimes he would choke as he tried to swallow it whole. I remember flying back to Michigan for Christmas that year. We had a layover and had just enough time to eat some lunch. James had a few jars of baby food while Jon and I ate at the restaurant. There was another young mother there with a little girl a bit younger than James.

"How old is he?" she asked.

"Nineteen months," I replied.

"Oh. He must be small for his age."

"Yes. He's only in the tenth percentile," I said. "How old is your little girl?"

"Eleven months," she said rather proudly as she handed her little pieces of bananas.

After some pleasantries regarding safe travels, we were back to eating our own meals. But I couldn't help but catch the gazes that the lady kept directing our way, especially as I fed James his baby food. I know what she was thinking because I have thought similar things many times, especially before I had a kid of my own, as I observe others in public places with their young children. *That child is* way too old *to be still eating baby food.* Perhaps she even thought, *No wonder he's so small.* It is amazing how just a glance can bear all the thoughts and judgments behind it and make the one being observed melt into insecurity, especially if they are on shaky ground to begin with. Not that I cared so much about what that particular lady thought. It was just that I knew she was right. I was feeling pretty sad about how far behind James was with his eating and his steps. I should have realized that things can always get worse.

As I recovered my strength from the illness, I noticed that it was becoming more difficult to get James to eat his baby food. After one particularly frustrating meal, I tried the airplane trick. The food flying around on the spoon before entering his mouth was a good distraction for a day or two, but by the third day, something even more entertaining was required. I discovered that James really enjoyed it when I cheered and clapped for him rather crazily after each bite. This also worked well for a couple of days, but with three meals and two snacks every day, feeding James was almost becoming a workout. And during these few days, he also decided to stop drinking.

I took him to the pediatrician, and he suspected he might be constipated and did an X-ray of his belly. Sure enough, James was pretty backed up. The doctor felt somewhat confident that if we could just clear him out, he'd be back to eating again. So we stopped at the drugstore and purchased all the various medicines that people take to prepare themselves for surgery or other more daunting procedures. These things worked to clean him out, and I think there was a day in there where he seemed to eat a little more than usual, but he still would not drink.

Several weeks went by, and the situation only got worse. I was monitoring James's wet diapers, and if he went more than eight hours without having a wet one, I would get out the syringe and put the water in his mouth drop by drop, like we had done before, and then massage the back of his jaw or even pinch his nose until he swallowed. I used this method for his food as well. I found that I could pry his mouth open if I squeezed his cheeks toward the back of his jaw and then dump the food in before he had a chance to snap it shut again. Thankfully, he never quite figured out how to spit out the pureed baby food like he had the chunkier finger foods. He did often store it in his mouth for five or more minutes before he finally swallowed and I could pry in the next bite. I was literally spending about half the day trying to feed him or get him to drink.

He was getting occupational therapy (OT) at the time, and the therapist was trying everything she could think of to help with his swallowing. The nutritionist from the early intervention program also came to see him several times. She advised me to start putting high-fat/high-calorie things in his food because it was clear that, once again, he was losing weight. So I put butter or olive oil in all of his little baby food jars. I bought a powder that was basically powdered fat and sprinkled it into everything. I even mixed his whole milk with heavy cream.

It was during these few weeks that we moved into our new house. Thankfully, we had movers who brought in all our boxes from storage, as I was basically just trying to keep James alive until we could get all of the papers signed, get the heat turned on, and at least put up our bed so we would have a place to sleep.

As we were moving in, the OT seeing James had given me a number for a special eating clinic in Winston-Salem. After one particularly long and tedious meal, I decided to escape the boxes. I put James in the car and drove to the pharmacy down the road, sat in the parking lot, and dialed the clinic. The lady on the phone was patient and understanding. I explained James's situation to her, and she assured me that they see kids in similar situations all the time and are really able to help many of them. The hope in me was building as I talked to her.

I was at my wit's end. I just could not figure out *why* James had stopped eating and drinking. I had tried everything I could think of. I had tried everything the OT and nutritionist could think of. I had tried everything that my family and friends had suggested. My personality is such that, when I am faced with problems, my answers have always been either fix it or shut up and live with it. But in this situation, I could do neither. And the situation only seemed to get worse as time went on. Convinced that this clinic was the best chance I had at that moment, I requested an appointment. Some time passed as the lady was looking through the computer for an opening.

"The soonest I can get you in is in five weeks."

"Five weeks!" I said. "But my son doesn't eat *today*. He hasn't been eating hardly anything for weeks already. I don't think he'll make it another five weeks."

"I know. I'm sorry," she said. "I wish I could do better. I can put you on our waiting list, and if we have a cancellation, you could get in sooner."

Does she really know? I thought. *When I said, "I don't think he'll make it," I really meant it. Is she really saying that it doesn't matter if my kid starves to death in the next six weeks, they simply can't accommodate me into their schedule?*

"How many are already on the waiting list?" I asked.

"Five or six, I think," she said.

And there was a long pause of silence on both ends of the phone.

"There is *nothing* else I can do to get in sooner?" I asked.

"No, I'm afraid not."

"Okay. Put me on the waiting list," I said and proceeded to give her all of my necessary contact information. With tears in my eyes, I pulled up to the drive-through window of the pharmacy and picked up James's seizure medicine.

I went to see the pediatrician again that week. James still had a bit of a constipation problem, but we were both in agreement that it was not the main issue. This wasn't a major side effect of any of his current medications like it was before. The doctor had run out of ideas. And James's height and weight had dropped down off the chart. In other words, he was lower than the zero-eth percentile, if that even makes sense. He had stopped growing and was losing weight. They scheduled an appointment for James to see the chief of pediatric gastroenterology and nutrition at Duke.

I know the specialty clinic can turn you away. But they can't do that to you at the hospital. At least they will have to try something, I thought as I drove the seventy-five-minute drive back to Duke for the new appointment.

Again, the hope in me began to build as I waited in the little clinic room for the chief of pediatric gastroenterology and nutrition to arrive. Surely with a title like that, this man was bound to have some ideas that no one else had thought of. Certainly there would be a key insight that would unlock the mystery of James's lack of appetite.

He listened very intently as I explained all that had transpired and the many things we had tried, shaking his head in understanding. "Well," he said, as I finished my story, "it seems clear that you really only have one option at this point."

I slid to the edge of my chair, anxious to hear the solution.

"You really should consider a feeding tube."

"A feeding tube?" I said, clearly surprised.

"Yes. Didn't your pediatrician tell you that it was probably what I would suggest?'

"No," I said, "he didn't. Isn't there any other option?"

"Well, it sounds like you have already tried all the other options."

My mind was whirling. I had recently met a lady who worked for our builder. Her daughter had a feeding tube. I had already questioned her extensively about it. I had also asked the OT about it, and from what I could tell, once you go down that path, it could be years before the child transitions back to eating orally. It starts out as a necessity, but then it can turn into a crutch. There is little motivation for the child or the parent to force learning to eat with their mouth. I was thinking that most kids get feeding tubes because they have a structural or medical issue with their throat or stomach. It didn't even occur to me that the doctor would suggest it for the child who simply refused to eat. Plus, James had eaten so well for over a year, so I knew there were no structural or medical issues. And it wasn't an issue of know-how. It seemed to be a matter of his will or his appetite. And how was that ever going to change if he was being fed from a tube?

I sighed and sat there thinking. The doctor waited patiently for my reply.

"No," I said. "No. I don't want to do that. Not yet. Two weeks. Give me two weeks, and if he's not eating better, then I'll come back and we can pursue it."

"All right," he said, with an understanding yet somewhat disassociated "your kid, your choice" sort of a tone.

Back at home, I hit my knees and asked others to do the same. Not that I hadn't been praying all along. The difference was that now it was quite literally my only hope. I had come to the edge of my own knowledge and abilities, and there was nothing left to do but pray and wonder why. *Why, God, after doing so well with his eating, has James taken such a backward step? I didn't get too mad when we had to move. I had set my mind so diligently on teaching him to walk, being disciplined with practicing. Why did You give us this huge problem that has completely derailed that effort?*

The first week of the two transpired basically the same way that the preceding weeks had, but as the second week began, it seemed to get somewhat easier. James was starting to eat the first two or three bites of a meal without protest. I kept experimenting with different foods, hoping to find one he really liked. I never found one that stood out. But I did find some things that I know he really did *not* like and was able to avoid those. It wasn't as if he just woke up one day and started eating again. It was more like I woke up one day and *realized* that he was, in fact, slowly getting better. By the time the second week came to an end, he was by no means eating normally, but I could detect a significant change. Over the next three to four weeks, he ate more and more. We never went back to the gastroenterology doctor at Duke.

There were six weeks in all that James refused to eat anything. I don't know why. I never figured it out. And to this day, I'm not sure why he started eating again either. It took about nine months for his body weight to register back on the child growth chart.

Even when he did start eating, he did not start drinking. It would take more than a year before he started drinking significantly on his own again. For over twenty-one months, he never willingly drank more than 4 to 6 ounces of liquid a day. Thankfully, baby food is pretty juicy. Instead of milk, he ate yogurt. Instead of apple juice, he ate applesauce. For six of those months, I really worried about it. But one day, it just occurred to me, *Well, he seems to still be alive and doing well on four to six ounces a day. I guess I'll just stop worrying about it.*

Two months after we moved in to our new house, I called my mom with the computer's webcam.

"You have to see this, Mom," I said.

With both my mom and dad watching from Michigan, I stepped back from the computer and stood James up on his feet. Holding his two little hands by his wrists, I slowly leaned him forward. Without me touching his legs at all, but with a lot of verbal cues and encouragement, he extended his right foot. We slowly covered the small distance to the computer desk step by step as cheers came though the speakers.

But we have this treasure [the knowledge of God] in earthen vessels, so that the surpassing greatness of the power will be of God and not from ourselves...

2 Corinthians 4:7

The Lord has made everything for its own purpose...

Proverbs 16:4

Not only is God in control of every detail of our life, but everything in our life, including our trials, is part of a plan. It's hard to fully understand, and I'm not saying that I really do, but even in the chance events of our life (Luke 10:31), from God's perspective, there are no accidents. It's just that sometimes the details of God's plan for our lives are not quite the same as our plans. What seems good to us might not actually be the best good the way God sees it.

God is the Potter. We are just the clay. "On the contrary, who are you, O man, who answers back to God? The thing molded will not say to the molder, 'Why did you make me like this,' will it? Or does not the potter have a right over the clay..." (Romans 9:21-22a).

Lois Flowers, in her book, *Infertility: Finding God's Peace in the Journey*, shares about her struggles with infertility due to a bad case of endometriosis. The doctors had told her there was little to no chance of her conceiving on her own. But she and her husband decided to give it a try anyway. She writes:

Wouldn't it be neat if I got pregnant right away? I thought. *Wouldn't that be a real testament to God's power? He would definitely receive all the glory for performing such a miracle.* (Looking back, I

realize rather sheepishly that those musings were only the first
in a long line of such thoughts—as if I knew better than God
what He should do to receive glory in my life.)[8]

Haven't we all prayed that prayer? I love her comment, as if we
know better than God what He needs to do in our lives, not only
for His greatest glory, but also for our greatest good.

In Romans, we find the often-quoted promise, "And we know
that God causes all things to work together for good to those
who love God, to those who are called according to His purpose"
(Romans 8:28).

It's not that all things by themselves are good. Many things
that happen to us seem terrible at the time. And if we were
honest, many of them stay that way. Paul isn't saying that every
single event will be good but that God is orchestrating the events
in your life such that they will all work together for your greatest
good, even if some of those events on their own are not pleasant.

We might not ever discover the purpose behind a particular
trial. In these situations, we have the opportunity to exercise our
faith in His written Word, that there is a reason and the reason is
good. But sometimes God does reveal at least one reason.

My sister's friend's dad struggled with a chronic illness for
years, and it had become clear that the illness would soon take
his life. The family hoped and prayed that he would die quickly
and with as little pain as possible. But it turned out to be just the
opposite. As he struggled in pain at home, hospice sent a nurse/
therapist over to help their family. The man they sent led a very
openly sinful lifestyle and had rejected God completely.

As the weeks went by and their father suffered in his illness,
the man from hospice more or less lived with their family, taking
care of their father and observing their faith. One particularly

difficult and painful day for their father, the family sat around his bedside and sang quietly the song "Jesus Loves Me." After the song finished, the man attending to their father broke down before them and admitted that he needed a Savior. He accepted Christ that day, and the very same day, their father went home to be with the Lord.

Every pain has a purpose. God has a plan for your life; He "predestined [you] to become conformed to the image of His Son..." (Romans 8:29).

TRUST IN THE LORD WITH ALL YOUR HEART, AND DO NOT LEAN ON YOUR OWN UNDERSTANDING

Proverbs 3:5

Not again, I thought as I felt James's forehead with my hand and then bent down to give him the kiss test. His skin felt pretty warm to my lips, so I took his temperature. Sure enough, it was 100 degrees. It wasn't a significant fever, but I knew I'd better act fast with the Tylenol. Any sort of fever gave James seizures. He had been sick eighteen of the twenty-eight days of February, and I was so relieved when we had entered March. I couldn't wait for winter to be over.

Shortly after we moved into our new house and seemed to have the eating issue behind us, the neurologist suggested we try to wean James off one of his medicines and replace it with another. This particular medicine was good for babies, but many mothers reported that their child's cognitive function and general awareness and ability to learn increased when they were taken off it. Now that James had started taking some steps with our help and was showing interest in toys and other types of learning, I was anxious to give it a try.

Five days after we made the first small decrease in the medicine, he had eight seizures. But eventually, he adjusted and was fine. His seizures continued to be the same type he'd been having since the day he was born. They would last anywhere from twenty to sixty seconds. He would get a bit stiff and stare off into space with a sort of scared look on his face.

The second time we decreased his medicine five days later, he had twenty-seven seizures over a four-day period, but then he was fine. I hesitated to decrease it a third time, but the possible benefits of increased cognitive function made me try again. And here it was, five days later, and he was running a fever.

I watched him closely throughout the day, and he didn't seem to act sick. Then, to my great surprise, during his afternoon snack, he actually drank five whole ounces. I was grateful if he would drink four or five ounces over the whole entire day. I was so excited to see that he had drunk that much all at once.

As I cleaned up from the snack, I noticed out of the corner of my eye that James was lying on his back on the living room floor, clearly having a seizure. I rushed over to him to hold him and make sure I was there to hug him and give him comfort when he came out of it, expecting it to last the typical twenty to sixty seconds. But sixty seconds passed, and he was still seizing. Then another minute went by, then two, then three. As the minutes ticked away, I also noticed his breathing becoming more like intermittent gasps.

About five minutes into the seizure, he stopped breathing completely. I waited maybe another minute for him to take a breath, but he did not. I ran for the phone and was back in the living room, hunched over James as I dialed 911. The phone started ringing in my ear, and I noticed James's body starting to get pale, and the pink around his lips was turning an ashy blue. Forgetting almost everything I knew about CPR, I pinched his little nose, put my lips to his, and pushed a small breath into his mouth as the lady on the other end of the phone said, "911, can I help you?"

"My son is having a seizure, and he's not breathing!" I said as I breathed once more into James's open mouth.

"Okay," she said in a rather exaggerated calm voice. "Do not attempt CPR."

Too late, I thought but didn't have time to say because James started coughing.

"I think he's coming out of it!" I said.

She assured me that the ambulance was on its way, and within two minutes, I was hanging up the phone with her because my doorbell was ringing.

I picked up James's limp body and went to the front door. It was the volunteer fireman from down the street. He had heard the call on his radio and decided to come because he was so close. But by then James looked like he might be recovering. I was explaining to the man James's condition as I held him in my arms when he started seizing again. I put him down on the rug in our entryway to try to keep him more stable as another truck pulled up to the house. It was another volunteer fireman, but this man brought some equipment. First, he took James's little finger and measured the oxygen saturation level in his blood. It should be close to 100 percent. His was 64 percent. Thankfully, the second man had oxygen with him, and he put the gigantic oxygen mask over James's little face. He was still seizing when the ambulance arrived a full twenty minutes after I made the 911 call.

"What medicines is he taking?" said one of the six men who were now gathered in my entryway.

"What is his diagnosis?" said another.

"How long has he been like this?" said yet another.

"Ma'am, can you come over here and try to get his attention?"

"What hospital do you want us to take him to?"

"What is his insurance information?"

Two minutes after the first ambulance arrived, another two were right behind it. Including the truck the fireman came in, there were now four vehicles with lights flashing in front of our house. Perhaps as many as eight or ten men now moved around inside our entryway, continuing to fire question after question at me as I looked down at James's face, still breathing, this time under the oxygen mask. His eyes were open, but he clearly was not there.

The paramedics worked on James for another ten minutes, during which time I was able to call Jon and briefly tell him what was going on. I don't really know what the paramedics did during that time other than get all his vital signs and fill out papers. I think they were waiting for him to stop seizing, but he never did. Finally, they decided to move him out to the ambulance. I went out ahead of them and climbed in the front seat. I dialed my mom on my cell phone as I watched a large man carry James's little body out to the back of the ambulance.

"Mom, it's James! He's having a seizure, and it won't stop! He's been having this seizure for over a half hour now. I'm in the ambulance, and we're going to the hospital. Please pray. Just pray! I'll call you back," I said and slapped the phone shut.

With the ambulance parked on the street in front of our house, the paramedics gave him some sort of rectal medicine and waited again for the medicine to stop his seizure. It did not. The man who carried James out was talking on the radio, with the doctor back at the hospital I guessed, and he decided to bring him in. The back doors of the ambulance were shut, and I looked out the window and saw everyone in my entire neighborhood standing in their front yard, watching as we sped away, sirens blasting.

Why do we live so far out in the country? I was asking myself as we made the thirty-minute drive to the hospital in a record twenty minutes. *Lord, please don't take him from me! Lord, please help him come out of this seizure! God, please, please, please do not take my little boy!* I prayed the entire way as I shifted my gaze from the road to the back of the ambulance, where James lay strapped to the gigantic gurney, his little arms and legs raising up and down now in a jumpy, pulsing action.

I can't remember if the paramedic in the back of the ambulance started an IV before we left or whether it was on the way to the hospital. But sometime before we arrived, he had given him valium through the IV. That did not work either.

We pulled up under the canopy of the ER and rushed in. Once inside, I stood at the side of James's bed, watching his little body continue to jump up and down as the doctors asked a series of questions about his condition, his recent seizure activity, his weight, etc. I'm not sure how many different medicines they put into him through that IV, but they continued to try things and then wait to see if they would work.

After about ten minutes, he did seem to calm down, but his fingers and toes continued to pulse. Another five minutes went by, and his fingers also stopped jumping, but his big toe continued to jerk up toward his head and then back down. I sat staring at that little toe for a few minutes more when I realized I should call Jon again.

I couldn't get a signal in the room where we were, so I went outside of the curtained area and stood near the door, where I was able to make the call. I was explaining to Jon what had happened in the past twenty minutes, when the doctor came rushing around the corner and said, "He's stopped seizing, I think. His little toe has stopped moving." I passed the word on to Jon and hurried back to James.

Faith is the assurance of things hoped for. What things? The things that God has told us, revelations we can think of as promises because God will always keep His word. And we can be absolutely certain of these promises because they are written and recorded in Scripture. God is in control of every detail of your life. He knows what you are going through. He loves you with an unfailing love. Every pain has a purpose. God has a plan specifically for you. And God is completely trustworthy. "For He Himself has said, 'I will never desert you, nor will I ever forsake you'" (Hebrews 13:5b).

The author of Hebrews is quoting from Joshua chapter one. The people of Israel had been wandering in the wilderness for forty years, suffering hardships and distress beyond what any of them could have imagined. During that time, almost everyone over the age of sixty had died. When they had come to the edge of the promised land, their great leader, Moses, died. Joshua took over the leadership of the people, and God gave him a promise: "Every place on which the sole of your foot treads, I have given it to you... Just as I have been with Moses, I will be with you; I will not fail you or forsake you" (Joshua 1:3-5). In verse 6, God said to Joshua, "Be strong and courageous." In verse 7, He said, "Be strong and very courageous." In verse 9, He said, "Have I not commanded you? Be strong and courageous! Do not tremble or be dismayed, for the LORD your God is with you wherever you go."

God had made Joshua a promise. And He made it clear that He would not forsake Joshua. He would not abandon him. He would not dissert him. He would keep His promise. Do you think it was easy sailing for Joshua after that? Do you think he just walked though the land, victory after victory, everyone just laying down their weapons and saying, "Come on in. Take our land. We know it has been promised to you." Of course not! There was a reason God told him three times to be strong and courageous. He was going to need it. The book of Joshua is perhaps the bloodiest and most intense and dramatic book of the Bible, filled with war and trial and plenty of close calls. God told Joshua that he should have courage, not because of his own strength, but because God would go with him everywhere he went.

In the last chapter of Joshua, after all the battles had been waged and the land was divided among the people, it says, "Then Joshua dismissed the people, each to his inheritance. It came about after these things that Joshua the son of Nun, the servant of the LORD, died, being one hundred and ten years old" (Joshua 24:28-29). God kept His promise to Joshua. And He will keep His promises to you. We need to be careful about Old Testament promises because they don't always apply to us, but in this particular case, we know from the book of Hebrews that God makes the same promise to us that He did to Joshua: He will never desert us! And He is completely trustworthy.

> Trust in the LORD with all your heart
> And do not lean on your own understanding.
> In all your ways acknowledge Him,
> And He will make your paths straight.
>
> Proverbs 3:5-6

"In all your ways acknowledge Him." To acknowledge means to perceive, to recognize. Realize that in *all* the things you do, God is there—in the good times and in the bad. Trust Him, recognize His hand in all you do and in all that is done to you. Lean on His promises, not on your own understanding.

Remember, proverbs are truisms, not promises. They are general social truths but not individual guarantees. What the author is saying is that by acknowledging God in your trial, you are likely to have straight paths.

In all, James's long seizure lasted about seventy minutes. It was the beginning of a whole new type of seizure for him. Three days later, when leaving the hospital, we were given a prescription for Diastat, an emergency medicine specifically to be used for long seizures. Everywhere James went, the medicine would have to go with him. I no longer felt comfortable being more than twenty minutes from a hospital. As it turned out, God wasn't done working on us yet. There was still so much left to surrender to Him, still so much trusting yet to do. Our age isn't characterized by God talking directly to us, as He did in Joshua's day. But perhaps if it was, I would have heard, "Be strong and courageous!"

DO NOT REGARD
LIGHTLY THE
DISCIPLINE
OF THE LORD

Hebrews 12:5

I'm often surprised by how quickly we can become comfortable, even in the most extreme conditions. Only one week after James's long seizure in March 2005, he was back in the hospital with rotavirus. He was literally throwing up every ten minutes for about eighteen hours straight. I couldn't give him his seizure medicine, and he became very dehydrated, so we went back to the hospital and stayed three days.

He had several seizures in April, and on April 30, he had forty seizures in one day. Again, we were back to the hospital. On May 18, I woke up in the early morning hours because James was having trouble breathing and couldn't stop coughing. This time, it was croup that once more brought us to the hospital. During all these months, he never went more than a week or two without seizures.

Looking back over my calendar at all of those separate, rather traumatic events of that spring, I don't remember much about what I was thinking during that time. I don't remember feeling extremely hurt or tired or scared. I don't remember learning anything truly profound about God or myself. To say that I took it lightly wouldn't be quite correct, because how could someone ever take such things lightly? But I had gotten into a groove. I knew how to respond well to an emergency. I was able to administer medication in more ways than I had ever imagined I would. I was becoming comfortable in the suffering servant role. I knew how to trust God in a crisis. I wasn't reflecting on the tough times much, however. I was just responding and trying to stay focused on the positive.

Even though James was two years old, he couldn't say any words, but we were trying to teach him sign language. Several months earlier, he had mastered the sign for *more*. In fact, he used it for everything. So much so that I was pretty sure he had no idea what the word actually meant. He just knew that he could get a response out of me when he did it.

"James, do you want to look at this book?"

More.

"James, is this block red?"

More.

"James, we're going to go outside for a walk."

More.

"James, do you want some crackers?"

More.

"I love you, James!"

More.

I was working with the speech therapist, trying to get him to understand opposing concepts and the sign for "all done." The perfect learning tool for this was his stander. He wasn't too fond of that thing.

Thanks to a forward-thinking physical therapist he had back in Raleigh, we were able to get the unique piece of equipment when James had Medicaid. He was really too small for it at the time, but later, it was a perfect fit. There were two plates with heel cups that he stood on and then a series of large Velcro straps that synched around his knees, hips, and waist, holding him upright. It was great exercise for his little leg muscles and good for his bones to have some weight bearing. We started him out in it for only a few minutes but were slowly working up to twenty minutes of standing.

Every time I took him out, I would tell him, "James, all done with the stander," as I made the motion for the "all done" sign. Many days he would respond with the *more* sign while at the same time clearly expressing his desire to be all done.

It took about twelve weeks of constant input before one day I approached him in his stander to get him out and he reached up with his little hands and signaled *all done.*

"That's right, James! All done!" I yelled as I jumped up and down and clapped my hands.

Clearly pleased with himself, he signed again, *all done.*

He always responded well to overly dramatic encouragement.

I had tried to teach him so many things over the months but had given up because he just didn't show any progress. But this new sign gave me renewed hope.

He can *learn,* I thought. *It just takes about ten times longer than you expect it to.*

One particularly sunny June day, late in the morning, I went to get James out of his stander. "Are you all done with your stander?" I asked.

All done! he signed.

I didn't realize that you can express attitude in a sign, but you sure can.

I unstrapped him from the stander and put him in his high chair for lunch. Because he had just turned two, the milestone had opened up a broader range of safe food choices for him. Still anxious to give him high-fat and calorie-loaded foods, I thought I'd try peanut butter. After his normal lunch, I placed a small lump on the end of a spoon and offered it to James. As expected, he had no intention of trying something new. He used his newly acquired *all done* sign. But in an action that had become rather typical behavior for me when it came to food, I pried his little mouth open and put the spoon, peanut butter side down, on his tongue so he could get a taste. A small portion of what was on the spoon came off into his mouth, and he managed to push the spoon back out with his tongue.

I smiled as I watched him try to figure out what to do with the small lump of peanut butter that was still in his mouth. He didn't seem to mind the taste, but his expression turned quizzical as he repeatedly opened and then shut his mouth, waiting for the funny stuff to somehow dissolve or become dislodged from the roof of his mouth. Several minutes later, he seemed to have swallowed what little was there without too much of a fuss, and I took the spoon into the sink, satisfied, thinking that we'd try a bit more again the next day.

I took advantage of my time at the sink and proceeded to load a few dishes into the dishwasher when, from the living room, I heard the strained breathing and that crouplike cough that I had become so familiar with the month before. Running back into the living room, I bent down over James for a few minutes and just watched as his eyes began to tear up and his nose started running.

I don't have any food allergies and wasn't that familiar with allergy symptoms. I was still thinking about the croup that he had the month before, but certainly that hadn't come on this fast. I called the pediatrician at Duke. The nurse on the phone said it sounded like an allergy and that I should give him some Benadryl and bring him in to the nearest ER or urgent care center right away. I didn't have any Benadryl at home, so I hung up with her, put James in the car, and headed down the street to the pharmacy.

On the way there, I called my sister and asked her to look up the phone number of our new pediatrician in Greensboro on the Internet. I had recently switched to a local doctor, but I didn't have their number programmed into my cell phone yet, which was why I called Duke. I gave her the name of the doctor as I pulled up to the store, telling my sister I'd call her back for the number in a minute. I rushed into the store, found the Children's Benadryl, and gave James a dose before we even left the store.

By the time I was buckling James back in to his car seat, his face was beginning to look like something out of a sixties mutant horror movie. His upper lip was at least three times its normal size. His left eye was swollen completely shut, and his right eye wasn't far behind. His nose was bulbous and swollen, and bright-pink blotches emerged along his cheeks and down the sides of his neck and onto his chest. His nose was running quite a bit, and his breathing was still very crouplike, but he was clearly still able to get breaths in. I started down the road on my way to the nearest urgent care center, which was a good ten to twelve minutes away, and called my sister to get the number for the new doctor.

Knowing nothing about a peanut allergy, I was thinking that perhaps our old doctor's office was just being extremely cautious, not wanting to risk getting sued or blamed if some low probability event were to take place. I had grown accustomed to this "cover yourself" approach that most of the medical community find themselves bound to take, and I was anxious to get a second opinion.

As I drove on, one eye and ear on James and his breathing, one eye on the road, and one ear to the phone, I discovered that I was calling the new doctor's office over their lunch hour and was instructed by the recorded voice to call a different after-hours nurse line instead. I called the number and talked to a triage nurse for about thirty seconds and was put on hold for about five to ten minutes. Just as a different nurse came back on the line, I was pulling into the urgent care center. I explained the situation to the second nurse.

"How long ago did the reaction start?" she asked.

"I would say that it's been about twenty minutes ago now," I said.

"Why have you waited so long to call?" she said in a rather harsh and judgmental tone.

My mind wandered. How could I explain to her what the past few months and few years, for that matter, had done to me? How could I explain that I knew all too well what it was like to hold my child in my arms and think that this might be it, he might be dying. How could I explain to her that I knew what that was like and I knew that this wasn't it? I decided to tell her that I was switching pediatricians and that I had called the old one first because that was the number I had in my phone. I explained that I was sitting in the parking lot of the urgent care, trying to decide if I should go in.

She acted frustrated and said something along the lines of, "Why are you calling me then?" but moved on and asked if James was having trouble breathing.

"It doesn't sound like it anymore. He's still pretty swollen, but the swelling is starting to go down and his breathing seems to be getting better," I said.

"If you ask him, does he say that he feels better?" she asked.

"I don't know. He doesn't talk yet," I said, cringing because I knew where this line of questioning would eventually lead.

"*How* old is he?"

"He just turned two," I said. *Okay, here we go*, I thought. I really didn't want to have to go through all the details of James's medical condition with this lady.

"Can you just ask him if his tummy hurts?"

"No. He won't understand that. He has some developmental delays."

"What is his diagnosis?"

"Well, he doesn't really have one," I said as I tried to explain as quickly as possible the condition of James's brain and the associated symptoms, including the epilepsy.

But I knew at that point that I had already lost. Perhaps if you have a typical child, a call-line nurse would be willing to entertain actually making an objective assessment over the phone. But if you have any sort of unique health issue, there is no way you're getting past the "cover yourself" approach. It was clear that this lady was no longer going to make an honest assessment. She was going to tell us to take every precaution. Not that I blame her or the system that was directing her, but the truth of it was that I was completely on my own to make the decision.

I hung up the phone and just sat there, staring at James, listening to his breathing and watching his chest move up and down. After sitting in the car for several more minutes, I decided that the immediate danger had passed. The Benadryl seemed to be working, and the swelling was starting to go down. As I drove home from the parking lot of the urgent care center, frequently checking on James in the rearview mirror, I was starting to recognize my little boy again.

We were able to get in to the new pediatrician for an appointment later that afternoon. I explained his symptoms to the doctor, and while they scheduled James for an appointment with an allergist to confirm, the doctor seemed pretty certain that he had an anaphylactic reaction to the peanut butter. They gave James several other medications, just in case he had another flare up later in the day, realizing the peanut butter was still in his system somewhere. They also gave me a prescription for the Epi-Pen Jr., an emergency shot of epinephrine, yet another thing that I would have to carry with me everywhere James went in case the potentially deadly reaction were to occur again.

"We often are not prepared for a certain discipline, and we think that there is no need for it... We think that we know our condition, but actually we do not. Only God knows us."[9]

Jon and I attended a weekend conference where one of the speakers taught that our spiritual life is not like being in the Boy Scouts, where you earn a badge for a certain skill and then you're done. It's not a series of checkboxes that we rather methodically move through during our lifetime. The speaker told us of a terrible tragedy that took his father's life when he was just five years old. And then he told of the perhaps even more devastating events of two years prior, when he held his twenty-one-year-old daughter in his arms and watched her die. "Didn't I already have the suffering badge?" he questioned at the time.

I do not want to begin to imagine that I know God's agenda. "Who can know the mind of God? How unsearchable are His judgments and unfathomable His ways" (Romans 11:33-35). I cannot say what God wanted me to learn through James's peanut allergy. I can only say what I did learn. I shall try to never assume that I have learned something fully. I will never check a box and say, "Yes, I've learned that lesson, and now I can move on."

Being a Christian means having a personal relationship with Jesus Christ. It is not about following a specific religion. Religion is a set of rules and behaviors that you obey so that you will be accepted by God. But if you have a relationship with Jesus, you are already fully accepted by God because of what Jesus did on the cross. There is nothing you can *do* to be *more* accepted.

Contrarily, if you are following a religion, then it's all about what *you* can do. Therefore, with religion, there is always a limit to what God can ask of you because you are limited in what you can do. But if you are in a relationship with Jesus Christ, there is nothing you can do to be more accepted. You are accepted by God; therefore, out of love for Him, you choose to obey and open up your life for Him to work through you. When we follow Jesus, there is no limit to what God might ask of us because it's not what I can do but what God wants to do through me. And God is not limited.[10]

Never underestimate God's ability and wisdom to take you to a whole new level of maturity in a certain matter. Never underestimate His desire to bring you, once again, to your knees before Him. You need to look at every hardship as if it *could be* discipline from the Lord. Certainly not all trials are discipline. But because we can never know for sure why a particular trial has come our way, we have to at least ask ourselves if this particular one might be discipline. We'll never know for sure this side of eternity, but every trial could be a great opportunity to learn something more about whom you are or learn something more about God. As Watchman Nee observed about trials, "We thought that we were absolutely for God. Now we discover that we are full of plans for ourselves. In fact, we are so full of these things that we can only fall on our faces."[11]

> My son, do not regard lightly the discipline of the LORD, nor faint when you are reproved by Him; for those whom the LORD loves He disciplines, and He scourges every son whom He receives.
>
> Hebrews 12:5-6

It is true that here on this earth, God will allow us to reap what we sow (Galatians 6:7), and it is quite possible that the trial you are facing could simply be the consequences of sinful behavior by you or someone close to you. But also understand that there is "no condemnation for those who are in Christ Jesus" (Romans 8:1). God's discipline is not punishment; it is correction. Discipline is training and education. It is God taking action in our lives to correct mistakes, to curb passions, to provide instruction that aims at increasing virtue.[12] And the result should be as the psalmist's: "Before I was afflicted I went astray, But now I keep Your word" (Psalm 119:67).

> All discipline for the moment seems not to be joyful, but sorrowful; yet to those who have been trained by it, afterward it yields the peaceful fruit of righteousness.
>
> Hebrews 12:11

We should be disciplining ourselves so that God doesn't have to. No one hopes to find themselves in the middle of some discipline from the Almighty. But if, in hindsight, you suspect that a particular trial might have been discipline, you will probably have an easier time being joyful about it. Not that you were happy about the trial itself. The joy comes in appreciating the outcome.

Do you want God to help you correct your mistakes? Do you want His help controlling your sinful passions? Do you want Him to instruct you in such a way that increases your virtue? Do you hope for the results of that discipline "the peaceful fruit of righteousness," even if it's going to hurt a little?

Hebrews says that *all* discipline at the moment seems sorrowful. It cannot happen any other way. Do you desire the best God has for you, or do you desire a trial-free life? Are you praying for God's best blessings in your life and seem to only be receiving pain and heartache? Perhaps the sorrow you are feeling is, in fact, God's best. Perhaps He's giving you what you said you wanted. The only question is, did you really mean it when you asked?

I have learned over the years that my husband lives in the future and mulls over the what-ifs to such a degree that when a difficult trial finally does occur, he has already dealt with it weeks before and moved on. On the other hand, it can be days or even weeks after an event before I fully process it and respond truthfully.

In the days following James's allergic reaction to the peanut butter, he had forty-four seizures over a six-day period. During those days, I just responded—one more thing to cause seizures, another medicine to dispense. It wasn't until several weeks later that I became frustrated with God.

God, I could handle having a child who is developmentally disabled. I could deal with a child who is legally blind. I could learn enough to take care of a child with a chronic illness. I could become content with a child who is unable to walk. I could learn to communicate with a child who cannot talk. And Lord, I prayed, *I could even deal with a kid who has a peanut allergy. But please tell me, why does my child have to have* all *of these things?*

I listened, but there was no answer, only a firm realization of what I had already come to understand. Even to this day, James's peanut allergy is a constant reminder for me. I am a work in process. God's not done with me yet. I was still having trouble trusting, still trying to understand why, and still searching for sight instead of resting in faith.

> Behold, how happy is the man whom God reproves, so do not despise the discipline of the Almighty.
>
> Job 5:17

LET YOUR
REQUESTS BE MADE
KNOWN TO GOD

Philippians 4:6

It was a Monday morning, and I began to stir just before my alarm was set to go off at 3:45 a.m. I had taken a sleeping pill the night before, but still it took me over a half hour to fall asleep, and I had been awake several times throughout the night. As I hustled through my shower, I noticed that my stomach hurt, and I couldn't tell if it was nerves or if I had just gotten up too early. We packed everything into the car the night before, so there wasn't much to do to get ready. With the cars warming up outside, my parents, Jon's parents, and Jon and I gathered in our kitchen to pray one more time.

As my dad was praying, I felt overcome with a great sense of belonging. As our family stood praying together, I really felt what it is like to be part of a larger family. It was as if all the others who had been praying so diligently for James over the past months were standing there with us as we laid our concerns out before God Most High. I've always known in my head that the body of Christ was like a big family. But at that moment, I truly felt the love and support of all of my brothers and sisters in Christ. It was as if, there in that kitchen, I was experiencing the best of what an earthly family can be, and it gave me a small glimpse of the potential that the body of Christ has and what a future we have awaiting us when we will all be a family together with our Father in heaven.

With our final petitions entered, the only thing left to do was to get James out of bed. The cold of the morning air made him stir, and by the time we had him buckled into the backseat of the car, he was fully awake. About two miles down the road, I decided I needed to sit in the back with him and climbed over the seat. I held his hand and kissed his cheek the whole seventy-five minutes to Duke University Hospital.

As we waited for James's name to be called, I felt tense yet fully prepared. After all, we had anticipated this day for several months and knew it was a possibility for him since the day he was born. From the beginning, the doctors had mentioned the possibility of a somewhat radical surgery called a hemispherectomy. If James's seizures were uncontrollable with medication, then this surgery might help. There were only so many medicines to try, and James had been on most of them. Still, some days, he was having as many as thirty to forty seizures in one day. While it was an incredibly complicated and delicate surgical procedure, the explanation was simple. They were suggesting we voluntarily remove the entire right half of his brain.

In the month that preceded our trip to the hospital, James had gone through a lengthy series of tests. There was the video EEG, where he spent about thirty-six hours in the hospital under video surveillance with twenty probes glued to his head. The MRI was done. The PET scan verified. All indications were that all of his seizures were coming from the small right side of his brain. And that side was experiencing very little normal brain activity.

We had ample opportunity with the surgeon to ask our questions.

"Will this affect his motor skills?"

"His left side will be permanently affected," the doctor told us. "Many kids are not able to open their left hand afterward, although it could get better over time as the other side of the brain adapts."

"Will his vision change?"

"He will no longer be able to see out of the left side of both his eyes."

"Will his personality change?"

"It shouldn't."

"Are we sure that this will stop his seizures?"

"No."

"Do we have any other better alternatives for treating the seizures?"

"Not really."

When our family arrived at the hospital, we secured an entire section of the waiting area where we had spread out various snacks, books, computers, and other items to keep us busy for the expected eight-to-nine-hour procedure. Some friends were even scheduled to bring us dinner that night.

The nurse led us back to the pre-op area where, only a week before, I had toured and received the complete step-by-step scenario of what to expect, everything from what James would be wearing and what tubes he would have to how much swelling to expect and for how long. The hospital couldn't have done a better job preparing us. Jon and I waited patiently as we answered all of the medical history questions and watched the doctors and nurses, dressed in hospital green, gather in the hall, giant hairnets on their heads and green booties over their shoes. One of the older doctors was spending quite a bit of time on the phone.

During the overly thorough pre-op appointment the week before, the family life specialist had informed me that there was a small chance that our surgery could get canceled if there wasn't an ICU bed available for James when he came out of surgery. They only have a limited number of beds and nurses, so if there are a lot of pediatric emergencies that come into the ER and take up the ICU beds the night before, then they won't be able to do the surgery. As I listened to her, I never even imagined that would happen to us. But then again, a lot had happened that I never would have imagined.

So there we all stood, James not having eaten or drunk anything since midnight, six doctors, three nurses, all heads covered, all ready to go, but there were no ICU beds. One brave young doctor finally came over and broke the news that Jon and I had already guessed. After another hour of waiting, the chief neurosurgeon had informed us that he had rescheduled James's surgery for Wednesday.

Within another hour, flights had been changed and plans rearranged, and we ladies were off to the mall. There were so many people praying for James that morning, and there we were, shopping. Jon's sister thought we were bound to get some good deals with all those prayers. I was anxious to give those who were praying an update, so I made my way to the Apple store and an Internet connection, where I was able to send off an e-mail informing all of our friends and family that the surgery would take place on Wednesday.

Monday and Tuesday were nice, relaxing days spent with our parents, and before I knew it, I was prying James's sleeping little body out of grandma's arms and putting him in to bed on Tuesday night. I knelt beside his crib like I had made a habit of doing every night for the past few months. All those days, my prayer was pretty much the same: *Lord, please keep him safe through the surgery. Let it work to stop his seizures. Please provide for no complications, and please, please, Lord, do not take him from me.*

But that night, my prayer was different. Had I not just been in this place two nights before? Should I offer up yet another plea? I knelt there for a time, wondering just what specifically I should pray. And as I started to talk to the Lord, it slowly occurred to me what I must do.

Has it really come to this? I thought. *Can I really be this strong and mean it when I say it? You'd better not even say it, Debbie, if you don't really mean it.* With tears welling up in my eyes I prayed, *Lord, I put my little boy completely in Your hands. If You want to take him, then take him. He is Yours, not mine. I trust You completely, and I will honor You whatever Your will might be.* It was the hardest prayer I have ever prayed.

I climbed into bed and went right to sleep and slept soundly until my alarm clock woke me the next morning. As we drove to Duke for the second time, I noticed that I had forgotten a few of those things that I had thought were so critical to bring the first time. We didn't pray in the kitchen like we did before, but I didn't mind because that day, that second time, for the first time, I was fully prepared. I don't know why James's surgery was postponed like that. Perhaps I will never fully know, and I'm sure it wasn't just all about me. But I'm thankful that it was postponed.

That peace lasted all throughout the surgery and for the full six days that we were in the hospital afterward. It started to fade after time as we got home and back into the mundane things of life. Of course, I had the peace that I always have, trusting God in my normal fashion. But that just isn't the same as it was that night.

I know that there were so many brothers and sisters praying for safety for James that day, and I am so incredibly thankful to be able to write that he came though the surgery safely. And while we didn't yet know whether the procedure would be effective to stop his seizures, it did seem that there were no major complications. I know a lot of those dear friends were also praying for Jon and for me. I certainly do not imagine that the courage and peace that I felt during those days came from inside of me. It came down from above, like soldiers standing around me, guarding my heart and my mind—soldiers sent in response to all of those prayers.

Be anxious for nothing, but in everything by prayer and supplication with thanksgiving let your requests be made known to God. And the peace of God, which surpasses all comprehension, will guard your hearts and your minds in Christ Jesus.

Philippians 4:6-7

Thank God for do-overs. He doesn't always give them, but you must admit that even when we don't do it right the first time, so many times we get an opportunity or two (or sometimes three) to do better next time.

James had his first brain MRI since his birth the summer of 2005. We had at one time hoped that his right side would grow and begin to look more normal, but in the two years since his birth, there had been no change. His left side was still two or three times as big as his right side. It was very hard to tell which parts of his brain were healthy and which were damaged, so we were told that the hemispherectomy surgery would be even more complex than on a typical brain. We prayed and prayed that the medicines would work to control his seizures so that he would not have to have the dangerous surgery. But each month that passed, he had more and more seizures, and by January 2006, it seemed clear that surgery was inevitable.

Sometimes our prayers are answered the way we'd hoped, and sometimes they are not. Clearly, God's will will be done. God will have His way, no matter what we say. So how should we pray? And for that matter, why should we pray at all?

Why Pray?

In Philippians, Paul says that in everything, we are to bring our requests to God. In 1 Thessalonians 5:17, Paul says, "Pray without ceasing." Clearly, God wants us to pray. He has even commanded us to pray. When we choose to follow Jesus, we enter into a relationship with God Himself, and the key to maintaining any healthy relationship is communication. God speaks to us through His written Word. We communicate to Him through prayer. Prayer is much more than just posting a wish list, like children send to Santa each year. Prayer is growing and maintaining a relationship.

I recently returned from another girls' weekend with my roommates from college. This was our ninth year in a row of spending a long weekend together. Various people ask us what we do on these weekend trips, and most of the time, the answer is *nothing*. One year, we went to the beach, and we didn't even leave our room until 4:00 p.m. We just sit together and talk all weekend long. Sometimes we talk about nothing important. Sometimes we share frustrations or difficulties. Sometimes we laugh at life's embarrassments. And sometimes we celebrate God's blessings. Every year, I leave knowing these precious girls more intimately than the year before. I know they love me because I can tell them story after story of what is going on in my life and they sit and listen with interest and concern. God is also ready to listen if we would just talk to Him.

Another reason to pray is because it can be effective. In Luke 11:5-13, when Jesus was asked by His disciples to teach them to pray, Jesus gave the Lord's Prayer (a brief version of it is recorded in Luke), and then He told a story about a man who received food from a reluctant neighbor when he persisted in asking for it. Then He concluded by saying, "If you then, being evil, know how to give good gifts to your children, how much more will your heavenly Father give the Holy Spirit to those who ask Him?" (Luke 11:13).

In this instance, Jesus is specifically talking about the Father giving the Holy Spirit, which is certainly a good gift. It seems that Jesus was teaching that the effectiveness of your prayers can depend on *what* you're asking for, as well as your persistence in asking. In Matthew 7:7-8, Jesus made the point that our heavenly Father wants to give us what we desire when our desires are good. (See also Matthew 7:7-11 and Hebrews 11:6.)

The Bible also teaches that the effectiveness of our prayers can depend on the amount of sin in our life. James 5:16b says, "The effective prayer of a righteous man can accomplish much."

In Egypt, the Israelites cried out to God to be freed from their continual suffering, and God heard their prayers. (Exodus 2:23-24; 3:7). After many years in bondage, He sent Moses. The fact is that God does hear our prayers. And while we can never presume to control God with our prayers, many times He does choose to give us that thing we've been seeking. But even if He does not, the time spent on our knees is not lost. It builds and strengthens our relationship with God, and it is being obedient to a command (Jude 1:20).

For years Jon and I had prayed and prayed that James would not have to have such a dangerous surgery. God did not grant us that request. But all the heartfelt time that I spent with Him through those months in prayer were part of what helped me through the weeks and days preceding the surgery.

How Should We Pray?

In general, the Bible teaches us how to pray more by example than by a list of how-tos.

It's good to ask others to pray for you, as the author of Hebrews did (Hebrews 13:18-19; see also Romans 15:30-32 and 2 Corinthians 1:11). We can ask God for help with problems that don't have any apparent earthly solution (Exodus 17:4). Biblical prayer includes requests for God's help, even if our sin is what caused the need for help (Judges 2:18). When we pray, we can pray for the prayers of others (1 Kings 8:22-54). And it is biblical to ask God to respond according to His own character (Daniel 9:18-19).

If we look at the life of Jesus as our model, as is always the case, we can find some good answers on how to pray during times of trial. Jesus spent much time in prayer, both in public and in private. You might want to pray for lengthy periods of time before a big decision. Jesus spent all night in prayer before He chose His twelve disciples (Luke 6:12). Jesus took a few close friends on a prayer retreat when He went up the mountain to be transfigured (Luke 9:28).

If we look at just His most difficult day, the day of His arrest and crucifixion, we see Him praying with His close friends, praying alone, and praying in front of the crowd. Where was it that Jesus's sweat became like drops of blood? Not in Pilate's hall, nor on His way to Golgotha, carrying His own cross. It was in the garden of Gethsemane. Being grieved, He went there and "offered up prayers and supplications, with vehement cries and tears to Him who was able to save Him from death" (Hebrews 5:7). He knelt down, prayed for over an hour three times (possibly three hours) with great intensity, yet still He knew that His prayer requests would not be granted (Matthew 26:39, see also Matthew 26:36-46; Luke 21:36 and 22:41-44).

Prayer is something we are commanded to do. It builds our relationship with God, and it can be very effective. Even if it takes a disciplined effort or if you have to come to God with sweat and tears, you will never regret the time you spend in prayer.

WHY DO YOU HIDE YOUR FACE FROM ME?

Psalm 88:14

Two weeks after James's hemispherectomy surgery, we returned to the neurologist for a checkup. The same gray-haired doctor with the big, fuzzy beard and the flannel shirt—the one who talked to us so grimly the day James was born—now sat across from us with optimism.

"He seems to be recovering well from the surgery. Do you want to go ahead and take him off one of his medications?"

I stared down at the cuff of the doctor's tan corduroys, just thinking. "So soon?" I finally asked.

"Well, we can wait a few weeks more, if you'd like," he said.

We discussed which medicine we should try to reduce and what the side effects of it were. All three of the seizure medications James was taking had the side effect of slowing down or reducing James's mental capabilities, but there was one in particular that seemed to have the largest doping effect. We decided to begin the slow process of weaning James off that medicine.

I left the doctor's office so excited about the potential changes that we might be seeing in James. Already, since the surgery, there had been some great improvements. It's not that his personality had changed, but we were just beginning to see more of it. He was starting to vocalize more and be more assertive with his desires. He had always been such a happy and content little boy, but now we were starting to see him laugh and squeal with joy at specific things that we knew made him happy. He had even started to drink more consistently than he had before.

The first week of the medicine reduction passed by without a single incident, and so the next weekend Jon and I decided to take James to the mountains for a weekend getaway. It was spring in North Carolina, and all the trees were in bloom. The pear trees were only barely hanging on to their carpet of little white flowers, and the dogwoods had just started to show their large white blossoms. All the grass had come alive from its winter dormancy, and everything looked so green. As we took the short two-hour drive up to the Blue Ridge Mountains, I couldn't help but reflect on how this surgery, like springtime, was going to bring new life and hope into our family. *We are starting a whole new chapter in our life*, we both hoped. Jon and I had always been weekend explorers before James was born, and we were so anxious for freedom from the seizures and the flexibility it would give us again to continue to explore.

We had a great weekend. We took James on a short hike in his backpack to the top of the mountains and had a nice picnic lunch. We drove up to the hot springs and all took a dip, including James. His incision was still healing, and he got tired at times, but for the most part, he enjoyed the trip as much as we did. Even to this day, James loves to go on trips with ma-ma and da-da. He's such a great traveler, and we are so thankful for that.

It wasn't until five weeks after the surgery that James had his first seizure. Before the surgery, he had been having multiple short thirty- to ninety-second seizures. But this post-op seizure was different. Jon had left for work, and James and I had just finished up breakfast when he started seizing. At first he acted the same as before. But after two minutes, instead of coming out of it, his arms and legs began to move up and down in a pulsing motion. After about four minutes, I decided I'd better give him the emergency medicine, and after doing so, I knelt; hovered over his little body on the living room floor, carefully observing his breathing; and waited another two long minutes before the medicine stopped his seizure.

I was nervous that this long seizure would lead right to another seventy-plus-minute seizure like the one that had taken place the year before when I didn't yet have the emergency medicine. But the medicine knocked him out pretty good, and for at least the next three hours, he slept.

I called Jon at work, and my heart was breaking to have to tell him the news. Trying to be optimistic with each other, we hoped that this was just one isolated event and that James's condition would continue to improve. Later, as James lay sleeping, I knelt down by his bed to pray.

Why, God? Why? Why put him through that big surgery only to have it not work?

I pleaded as the tears welled up in my eyes. I couldn't think of much else to say, and surely God knew how much my heart ached at that moment. But there were no answers. I felt no comfort or peace as I had at other times in the past.

Is God even listening? I thought.

The next week, James had another seizure that lasted nine minutes. And the week after that, he had another that lasted a full twenty minutes. I had been in communication with the neurologist after each seizure, and after the third one, he suggested we try a new medication. This new one did not have negative side effects as strong as the other one we had weaned James from.

Two weeks went by on this new medication, and we were again starting to get hopeful when I woke up at 6:00 a.m. to a strange rhythmic thumping sound coming from the monitor. I rushed into James's room to find him having another seizure. I scooped him up and hurried him in onto our bed, where Jon was still trying to wake up. I quickly gave him the emergency medicine, and after only a few minutes, James's little legs stopped pulsing up and down. However, he wasn't really responsive either. And he wasn't passed-out asleep like he had been before. I couldn't really tell if he had stopped seizing or not. Then he started to whine. At first it was more of a grunt. But then he started arching his back and making a more constant, almost-crying type of sound. After a few minutes of this, he started bending and almost kicking his leg back and forth as if he were in some type of terrible pain. Jon and I had never seen him do anything like this before. We quickly decided to drive him to the ER at our local hospital.

By the time we got to the ER, what looked like pain to us was starting to subside, and he was only occasionally kicking his leg and moaning. We explained to the doctor that he had a seizure and that this was new behavior and we couldn't tell if he was still seizing or actually in pain. But by the time we could fully explain the situation, he had stopped the strange behavior and was in the drugged sleep I had become accustomed to after giving him the emergency medicine. The doctors did a CAT scan, but when they saw how deformed his left brain was and that his right brain was missing altogether, they had no idea what to tell us and sent us home with orders to follow up with his normal doctor. So by 8:00 a.m., we were back at home, and Jon was showering for work.

Later that day, I had a short discussion with the neurologist from Duke, who told me to increase the new medicine some. The rest of the day passed by in a blur, and the next morning,

James was still acting weak and tired from the seizure and all the medication the day before. We laid low that day, but the medication increase was not effective, and by 4:30 that afternoon, he was seizing again.

I gave him the emergency medicine right away, put him in the car, and headed off to the ER. I don't think it was really necessary to go to the ER, but I was worn out. I knew if I kept him at home, then I would have to decide what to do next. But if I brought him to the hospital, then the doctors would decide. Some days I was stronger than others, and that day I just couldn't handle making all the decisions myself.

It was hard to buckle James into his car seat pulsing like he was. But I managed it and tore out of the driveway and down the road. I was halfway to the hospital when James stopped seizing and began to arch and twist in his chair again as he cried out in apparent pain.

When I arrived at the hospital, I parked the car and stared out the window toward the door to the ER. Memories of the day before came to me, and I began rolling over in my mind again and again how the doctors there were able to do nothing for James. They had no advice, no answers, no comfort. I climbed into the back of the car and sat next to James, trying to comfort him as best I could as he kicked his foot and arched his back while moaning in a soft cry. I decided to call the doctor from Duke.

Our normal doctor wasn't available, so I talked to another doctor in the practice who was guessing that the crying and back arching sounded like the post-icktile phase of a seizure. He didn't know for sure but thought that James probably wasn't actually feeling pain or really aware of what was going on. His brain was just recovering from the seizure. I hung up with the doctor and sat there in the parking lot of the ER for another twenty minutes, holding James's little hand, kissing him on the cheek, and pleading to God for it to stop as he whined and twisted in what looked to me to be pain before he fell asleep, exhausted. I pulled out of the parking lot of the ER and drove slowly home.

The only thing I could manage to do during the car ride home was call Jon and let him know briefly what had happened. Most of the drive I spent in a silent stare; no thoughts, no anger—just mental numbness. I didn't pray. God felt so far away.

My eye has wasted away because of affliction; I have called upon You every day, O LORD; I have spread out my hands to You...But I, O LORD, have cried out to You for help. And in the morning my prayer comes before You. O LORD, why do You reject my soul? Why do You hide Your face from me?

Psalm 88:13-14

If you walk with God long enough, there is no doubt you will go through a time, like the psalmist did, when you want God to feel near, but instead, it seems as if He is keeping His distance. A good friend once said it best when she said, "I feel like my prayers are bouncing off the ceiling." Is it normal to feel distant from God? Yes. The Bible is full of dedicated servants of God who, for a season, felt an absence of the nearness and comfort of God.

Abraham was seventy-five when God asked Him to move to the land that He would show him. God promised Abraham that He would make him a great nation through his descendants (Genesis 12:1-4). Abraham began a faith-based relationship with God in Genesis 15:6, after he was specifically promised a son. That promise was not fulfilled for at least another thirteen years, when Abraham was one hundred years old. As far as we know,

Abraham did not hear from God again about the promise during that entire time until the year Isaac was conceived.

As 1 Kings 19 begins, Elijah, the prophet of God, has just had an amazing victory over the prophets of Baal by calling down fire from heaven. He prayed for rain, and it rained. He slew all the false prophets and then outran evil King Ahab's chariots over twenty miles back to the palace at Jezreel. When he got to the palace, Jezebel, the queen, threatened his life. If I were Elijah, I'd be thinking that if I called on God and He sent fire from heaven and then I prayed for rain and it rained, a simple request for his personal safety and protection would yield a swift and sure response from God. But God was completely silent, and as a result, Elijah ran for his life.

Elijah ran from Jezreel in the north of Israel all the way to Beersheba in the south, over one hundred miles. He then journeyed into the wilderness for a day and continued on to Horeb, another hundred miles, to the mountain of God (1 Kings 19:8). It seems he was not instructed to go there, at least not by God (1 Kings 19:9), but was running because he felt alone and in trouble.

In a cave on Mt. Horeb, God finally did come to him. And when He came, did God give him words of encouragement or comfort? God only asked, "What are you doing here?" Then Elijah went outside and experienced a strong wind, an earthquake, and fire. But God was not in the strong wind, not in the earthquake, nor was He in the fire. He was in the "gentle blowing" that followed (verses 11-12).

It would have taken Elijah weeks to get down to the mountain. Certainly, the moment for God to make a big entrance had passed. If I were Elijah, I'd be thinking, "God, couldn't you have showed up back at the palace in Jezreel before I took the journey of my life that has left me weak and hiding in this lonely cave?" In fact, God didn't make a big entrance at all but was in the "gentle blowing." Sometimes God makes you live through the storm and the fear, and then when the right moment seems long past, reassurance from Him will show up in the most unexpected way.

In Psalm 13, David felt ignored and forgotten. "How long, O LORD? Will You forget me forever?" (verse 1) Four times in the first two verses of the Psalm, he asks, "How long?" Obviously, God had felt distant for some time. "Consider and answer me, O Lord my God" (verse 3). David didn't ask God to do this or that but only to consider his case. And then he seemed to change his demeanor quite drastically by the end of his prayer. "But I have trusted in Your lovingkindness; My heart shall rejoice in Your salvation" (verse 5). Sometimes prayer brings our hearts and minds in tune with what we know to be true about God and away from our present situation. In this case, David trusts in the promises of Scripture and in his own past knowledge of God. "I have trusted in Your lovingkindness," past tense. And he rejoices in His salvation, a future promise.

It's not uncommon or abnormal as God's servant to feel ignored and forgotten by God. Sometimes, and for some reasons that we might never know, our feelings do not line up with what we know in our heads, and God seems silent. But the truth is, "For He Himself has said, 'I will never desert you, nor will I ever forsake you'" (Hebrews 13:5). God Himself has made this promise, and we can stand on its truth.

During times when God seems to us to be distant, we can pray like David did. We can trust in what we know to be true about God, not what we are feeling in that particular moment. And we can rejoice in God's promises. We know that God loves us. We know He has made everything according to His great purpose. We know He is working everything together for our good. And we know we can trust Him.

But still, sometimes we wonder, *Have I done something wrong?*

If we are caught up in "fleshly sin," not abstaining from evil and holding fast to what is good, then we can "quench" or suppress the Holy Spirit in our lives, and as a result, God can seem distant (1 Thessalonians 4:1-8, 5:16-22; Ephesians 4:30). We could be wondering why God has left when, in fact, we are the ones who have walked away.

In Isaiah 49:14, the southern kingdom of Judah is on the brink of invasion by the Babylonians as judgment for their continued rebellion against God. "The LORD has forsaken me, And the Lord has forgotten me," they cry. But listen to God's reply to His stubborn and sinful people:

> Can a woman forget her nursing child and have no compassion on the son of her womb? Even these may forget, but I will not forget you. Behold, I have inscribed you on the palms of My hands; Your walls are continually before Me... Those who hopefully wait for Me will not be put to shame.
>
> Isaiah 49:15, 16, 23b

Even when God's distance is the result of our own sinfulness, God will keep His promises.

There could also be times when we are not caught up in some type of sin but are just in the middle of a difficult battle, as Elijah was, and God can seem silent. Look at Jesus, for example. As Jesus hung on the cross, rejected and despised by those He came to save, broken and in pain, He cried out to His Father, "My God, My God, why have You forsaken Me?" (Matthew 27:46). Even though Jesus was in the very center of God's will, doing exactly what He came to earth to do, God was silent toward Him. I can't even imagine what it must have been like to be hanging there on that cross and have God turn His back on me. Thankfully, I will never have to experience either that type of punishment or being forsaken by God (Hebrews 13:5). Jesus went there in my place. The bottom line is that God's behavior and His character do not change with our actions or our feelings.

But is there something we can do to bring God closer?

It's good to pray for wisdom, as David did, and ask God to consider your situation. Prayer can help us remember God's past faithfulness and can make us mindful (implying knowledge) of God's future promises (see also Psalm 102).

Still, it can seem as though God has forgotten you in the midst of a trial. It doesn't really seem to matter if the trial is of your own doing or not. In these situations, God's behavior is not determined by *your* actions or *your* feelings. His behavior is determined by His character. God will keep His promises.

Is *your* behavior determined by your character or by how you are feeling at the moment? Do you trust in God's promises, or do you trust in how close God seems to *feel* to you right now?

The Apostle Peter tells us, "The Lord is not slow about His promise, as some count slowness, but is patient toward you…" (2 Peter 3:9). If God seems slow in showing you how much He loves you, it could be because He's waiting patiently for you. Perhaps you need to learn something specific or your faith is being perfected (James 2:22) so that you can become the person He created you to be. Our job is simply to "be diligent to be found by Him in peace, spotless and blameless, regarding the patience of our Lord as salvation…" (2 Peter 3:14-15).

"Do not fall from your own steadfastness, but grow in the grace and knowledge of our Lord…" (2 Peter 3:17-18). *Steadfast* means firm in belief, determination, or adherence. Peter is urging us that during these distant times we are to stand firm, be determined, and *choose* to stand on what you know, not how you feel.

Next, he says we are to grow. To grow means to spring up and develop to maturity. In this case, we are to grow in knowledge and in grace. Take this distant time to grow your knowledge of God. Read your Bible daily. Seek godly input from other followers of Christ. Reflect on His grace, His merciful kindness that drew you to Him for your salvation.

And finally, we should check our inputs. This world is controlled by Satan, and he is constantly bombarding us through the media or through earthly minded friends whose only objective is to hurt and destroy us. Let us take Paul's advice when he said to the Corinthians, "Destroy speculations and every lofty thing raised up against the knowledge of God...Take every thought captive" (2 Corinthians 10:5).

IF I WANT HIM TO REMAIN, WHAT IS THAT TO YOU?

John 21:22

I am the middle child of three girls. My oldest sister is one year and twenty months older than me, and my younger sister is one year and eight months younger. There were some difficult times growing up, especially those high school years, being so close in age, but overall, it has been a great experience.

As we all grew into adulthood, married, and became mothers, we have been able to share our experiences with both the milestones and the mundane details of life in a sometimes humorous and other times tense but always completely honest and self-revealing sort of way—the type of vulnerability that comes with the unconditional love that only sisters can share. Our conversations have not always been pretty or righteous (although sometimes they have), but they have been true to life. And for this reason, my sisters are a good representation to me of what others are thinking but often do not say. And the things I have shared with them are a truer representation of my own heart, as I've said things to them that I wouldn't think of sharing with others.

One day I was talking with one of them on the phone in the car, and she was complaining about the attitude of her three-year-old son and a particular discipline struggle she was having, and she said something along the lines of, "You should be glad that you don't have a kid who talks back."

"You have got to be kidding me," I was tempted to reply. But I didn't say anything because I knew she was just letting off steam. And I knew she was talking more about what she didn't have at that moment than what I had. But she hasn't been the only one to say something along those lines to Jon or to me. And because of James's sweet, joyous, and mild-tempered demeanor, I'm sure that many have thought it.

I'm often completely dumbfounded when I find out that someone observing our lives is envious of one particular thing. Yes, perhaps the one thing they are observing is a great blessing, but taken our life as a whole, I'm not sure they would want to trade places with us. But then why am I so dumbfounded? Only because I am doing the same thing observing their "normal," healthy children and thinking that because of that *one* thing, surely their life is better than ours.

For example, several months after James's surgery, it had been a particularly slow week for his seizure activity, so I decided to take him out to the craft store. They were having a sale, and I had some little craft ideas I wanted to work on. But mostly, I just wanted to get out of the house.

I put James in his stroller and began browsing through the aisles, my mind wandering away at the possibilities with each new and interesting craft supply that I saw. But as I had become in the habit of, my ears and eyes were never completely out of tune with James.

I didn't get more than about three aisles into the store when I heard him making a strange noise. I jerked him around in the stroller so I could get a full view of him, and sure enough, he was having another seizure. I was so close to the door that I decided to drop the few items I had picked up and rush out to the car to give him his emergency medicine there. Being a rectally administered medicine, it was easier to give it to him while he was lying in the hatchback of our car than right in the middle of the aisle in the store.

As I rushed out to the car, you'd think that my mind would be on James and his seizure and if he was okay, but as I passed the checkout aisle, I observed all the ladies standing in line purchasing their items, and instead, I thought, *I wish I could stand in line right now and buy the things I'd picked out like they are doing. I can't even get out of the house anymore. I can't even go to a store and make it to the checkout.*

Why is it we always want the one thing we don't have?

You shall not covet your neighbor's house; you shall not covet your neighbor's wife or his male servant or his female servant or his ox or his donkey or anything that belongs to your neighbor.

Exodus 20:17

One year for Father's Day, I got my dad a wooden plaque that had the cowboy commandments burned into the wood, of which number ten was listed as, "Don't be hankerin' after another man's stuff." When you look at your neighbor with desire for a particular part of that person's life, you are really saying that God has made a mistake with what He's given you. It's called coveting. It is very tempting to do when you're in the midst of a trial. But it is destructive to you and can be destructive to your neighbor as well.

In one of Jesus's more popular parables, He tells of two sons. The youngest demanded his inheritance, so his father divided his wealth and gave each son his share. But the younger son "squandered his estate with loose living" (Luke 15:13b). After coming to a low point, where he was working as a common laborer feeding pigs and even desired the food the pigs were eating to fill his stomach, he decided to return to his father with a repentant heart. When the father saw his prodigal son, he rejoiced and ordered a great feast. But the older son became angry toward his father because he was never given a great feast. And to this anger, his father replied, "Son, you have always been with me, and all that is mine is yours."

This parable has many great applications for the repentant life and the rejoicing over one who returns to God. But there is also a great lesson in the perspective of the older brother. The older brother had been blessed with a comfortable living in the household of his father. He had servants, plenty to eat, and a comfortable place to lay his head. He had his complete inheritance still intact. Everything the father had was his.

On the contrary, the younger brother had nothing but memories full of mistakes and brokenness. Yet the older brother was angry with his father about the one thing that he didn't have. Notice the details of the older brother's complaint: "I have never neglected a command of yours and yet you have never given me a young goat, so that I might celebrate with my friends" (Luke 15:29). In other words, "Why does *he* get that and I don't when I'm the one who deserves it?" How arrogant and shortsighted. Yet if we were honest with ourselves, most of the time, this is the root of our own complaints. We should be very slow and thoughtful about telling God what we think we deserve (in fact, I don't recommend it at all). We tend to forget the evil we've done and only remember the good. Do we really want God to give us *all* that we deserve?

In John 21, Jesus appeared to His disciples for perhaps the third time after He had been raised from the dead. They had been fishing all morning with nothing to show for it when Jesus appeared on the shore and instructed them to cast their net on the other side of the boat. When they did, they brought in 153 large fish. After breakfast on the shore, Jesus singled out Peter and asked him three times if he loved Him, and after each of Peter's responses, Jesus replied by giving Peter the same task: "Tend/Shepherd my sheep." Then Jesus prophesied about Peter's death when He said, "When you grow old, you will stretch out your hand and someone else will gird you, and bring you where you do not wish to go" (John 21:18b). Obviously, Peter had some trials ahead, and Jesus was giving him some of the specifics. Given the information, Jesus's command was simple: "Follow Me!"

What is interesting is Peter's response. He looked around and saw John standing behind him, so he said to Jesus, "Lord, and what about this man?" I see children do this all the time. One is asked to clean up the toys, and their response is to look at the other one standing near and say, "What about him?" In other words, "He should be cleaning up too!" or "Why do I have to clean up and he doesn't?"

Recently, James and I were visiting with my two sisters and their six kids for a long weekend at a cabin in the Smoky Mountains. Half of us were sleeping in one room and half of us in the other room. When it was time to go to bed, one of my sister's kids was told that they would be sleeping in the room with their mom while James and I would be sleeping in the bigger room with some of the other kids, to which the child replied with great anguish, "Why do they always get to do everything?" As adults, we roll our eyes or perhaps even giggle when our children act this way. But then we turn around and do the same thing to God when we don't get our own way.

"Why do teenagers who smoke and drink while they are pregnant give birth to perfectly healthy babies whom they can't even care for while I took every precaution while pregnant and my child is the one with the major birth defect?"

"There are inbred alley cats that roam the streets that can walk better than my son. Why?"

"Some parents give their kids nothing but junk food and let them sit on the couch, watching TV all day, yet their kids are not in the hospital all the time."

"Some parents complain because it takes three months to potty train their kids. I've been taking James on and off that potty for over three *years* and he still is in Pull-Ups."

I could go on and on, and believe me, I have. Our adult desires might seem to be more important than what room we're sleeping in. But no problem is too simple for God to care about and no issue too difficult for Him to change, should He choose to change it. Let's see how Jesus answered Peter because He probably would answer our own questions in a similar fashion.

Jesus said to Peter, "If I want him to remain until I come, what is that to you? You follow Me!" Jesus wasn't saying that John wasn't going to die. Jesus was just saying that John's life was John's life and Peter's life was Peter's life. God isn't concerned about fairness. He doesn't give the same exact thing to everyone. Instead, He will give you exactly what you need in your situation to bring out the best in you, all for His glory. God treats us as individuals. We all have different sinful tendencies we need help working on and different gifts and talents we can offer. We each have a plan for our lives. My story is not the same as the pregnant teen's is. Her trial came about as the result of sin, while, at times, my response to my trial was sinful. But if she knows the Lord, God is writing a great story in her life too.

We don't have to be taught some of God's laws over and over again. Usually they are the ones we are not tempted to break. But others are trickier. For me, coveting has been a tricky one. On the surface, it seems so simple. Don't desire that great new house your friends just built. Don't envy that great new job that he just got promoted into. Don't wish that you had a great figure like she does. Stop envying how loving and kind her husband seems to be. Don't wish that you had the money for trendy and fashionable clothes like she does. Not that I haven't at one time or another wanted these things, but usually when these types of things enter my mind, I recognize them as coveting right away and can dismiss them for what they are. I ask for forgiveness and move on. They don't consume me.

But if you haven't at one time or another struggled with coveting, then chances are you haven't yet been deprived of something you *really* wanted or, worse yet, something you thought you deserved. It's easy for me to not covet another woman's husband because I think the husband I've got is pretty great. It's easy for me to not covet someone's great wardrobe because I've never really cared too much about what I wear.

As Watchman Nee said in his book, *The Breaking of the Outer Man and the Release of the Spirit,* "We often are doing God's will outwardly, but actually it is only a coincidence that God's will matches our will."[13]

In Romans, Paul writes, "I would not have known about coveting if the Law had not said, 'You shall not covet.' But sin, taking opportunity through the commandment, produced in my coveting of every kind..." (Romans 7:7b-8a).

I never really struggled with coveting until James was born. Was I actually *more* righteous before he came along? I don't think so. It's just that the new situation I was in had revealed my unrighteousness. My trial was not the result of sin, but my reaction to it was. All of a sudden, something had been taken from me that I really wanted, something I even thought I *deserved*: a healthy child. I didn't even realize I wanted it so badly until it was taken from me. Because of this trial, a bright light was shining on a very dark part of my life, an area that I needed to spend some time cleaning up. But I never would have even known that the dark spot existed if God hadn't, in His great mercy, shone His light on it by giving me this trial.

Maybe God is using your trial to expose an area of your life that you have not yet turned over to Him. What are *you* hanging on to so tightly? If you don't know, then you might be hanging on to it so tightly and for so long that you don't even realize it. But some of you, deep down, know exactly what I'm talking about. I'm not talking about tackling some type of overtly sinful behavior. I'm talking about these little idols we've erected in our lives that, on the surface, seem like good things but over time become more important to us than our relationship with God.

In Lois Flowers' book, *Infertility: Finding God's Peace in the Journey*, she makes this difficult but revealing statement:

> Perhaps you found yourself...saying... "I don't even want to entertain the thought that, in order for God's will to be done in my life, I might have to release my dream of getting pregnant and having a baby. I just won't do it. I want a baby too much."
> ...If this describes you; your biggest problem is not infertility. It's lack of submission to your heavenly Father.[14]

Looking back at John's description of the conversation Jesus had with Peter on the shore, John said that Jesus was describing or "signifying by what kind of death he (Peter) would glorify God." Is there no greater thing than to glorify God in our lives? Peter's trial was going to glorify God. Why would we run from an opportunity like that? Let us be grateful for everything that God has given us instead of wishing for what He has given our neighbor.

DESIRE REALIZED IS
SWEET TO THE SOUL

Proverbs 13:19

Jon and I have always wanted three children. As I said, I have
two sisters, and so does Jon, so we are accustomed to a somewhat
larger family. And while it wasn't always smooth sailing when we
were younger, we have really grown to appreciate our relationships
with our siblings now that we are adults.

Shortly after we moved to Greensboro, we decided to try to
have another baby. It was a tough decision because, at the time,
James was having a lot of seizures. He wasn't eating or drinking
well and was nowhere close to walking. Taking care of him was
certainly a full-time job, and it was hard for me to see how I could
manage another baby. But I was sure that most moms felt this
way before having a second child, even if their firstborn was more
typically developed. And so, as nervous as I was, I figured that
if others could do it, then so could I. I certainly wasn't going to
be the first mom of a child with special needs to go on and have
other kids. So in October 2004, we took the plunge.

Even though it had taken a whole year and a half to get
pregnant with James, I thought this time it might be quicker.
My oldest sister had taken an equally long time to conceive her

firstborn, and then, after only three months of trying, her second was on the way. I had another friend who had gone years without getting pregnant and then had two children almost back-to-back. So, armed with my sample size of two, I was convinced that my story would be similar.

The first two months were spent in anxious anticipation as I counted down the days to when my period would start. But by Christmas of that year, it was becoming increasingly apparent that James's seizures were spiraling out of control. And although we never put our baby efforts on hold, we had plenty of distractions as James began to undergo the long series of testing that led up to his hemispherectomy surgery in March.

After that first surgery, James had several more weeks of seizures, but when we got the new medicine up to a higher level, the seizures seemed to stop. We were so excited. The day James was born, he had a seizure, and then he had gone five and a half weeks before having his first seizure at home. Up until that summer, five and a half weeks had been his record. For most of his life, we were excited if he could make it just two weeks, which he rarely did. Looking back on his medical calendar, which I created to record his seizure frequency, medicine levels, and various test results, I see that in all of 2005, he never went more than three weeks without seizures.

During those seizure-free weeks following his surgery, I decided to go see my obstetrician. A friend had gotten me acquainted with a website that helps you try to predict the day you ovulate by charting your basal body temperature. The method was simple but somewhat laborious. Every morning before you get out of bed, you are supposed to use the special BBT thermometer and precisely record your temperature. Being an engineer, I was especially fond of this practice and enjoyed graphing the data in various ways on the computer, hoping somehow to glean some new insight that would provide the key to solving our problem.

I had been recording my temperature for several months when I went to my appointment with the OB, data in hand. We had been mostly preoccupied with James's surgery up until then, so I didn't feel too stressed about my inability to conceive. But at that point, I didn't want to mess around either. I knew my biological clock was ticking and if I wanted two more kids, I'd better get just a little help.

The OB took my blood to test my hormones and X-rayed my fallopian tubes with a dye running through them to make sure there weren't any blockages. My tubes were okay, but one of my hormones was a bit low, so she prescribed a drug that was supposed to help my ovulation. I took the pills for three months with no success.

Distracted by taking care of James, I never did follow up with my OB after taking the pills, and as time often does, over a year and a half flew by with no happy news. In February 2007, I determined that a new doctor was the answer and made an appointment with a reproductive endocrinologist at Duke. I remember sitting in the parking lot of the office with all sorts of hope. I had a close friend who had recently conceived through IVF (in-vitro fertilization), and I was pretty sure I didn't want to do that. Based on all the talking that tends to go on about this subject among my friends, I felt very informed. But I thought that surely there was something still unknown that would be appropriate for me to try that was somewhere in between just taking the hormone pills and stepping up to the $13,000-$20,000 IVF procedure.

I brought the results of all the previous testing, hoping I wouldn't have to repeat any of that. Our insurance did not cover any type of fertility treatment, and we had already spent a considerable sum on those tests.

The man was very patient, but I think I was more concerned with telling him what I knew than listening to what he knew. The appointment ended by him telling me that my best chance at conception was IVF. He gave me some different pills to try but basically told me to give him a call when I was ready for the IVF. I was terribly disappointed. I went in there thinking that the only thing I *didn't* want to do is IVF, and he was telling me that that was my only good option.

The new pills didn't work either, so the months ticked by, and I became even more uncertain about what to do. I was distracted through the fall with a mission trip to India in October, and then the holidays came and went and still no pregnancy. And then, one late winter day of 2008, I happened to hear a friend talking about her own fertility efforts, so I shared with her my struggles over the past three and a half years, and we had a good discussion about it. She seemed happy with her doctor, something I had yet to achieve. So I decided to try a new doctor once again.

Armed with all of my test results and various data, I met with the new doctor. I had learned at least a little bit from my last encounter and decided to keep my mouth shut as much as possible and try to learn from this man I was paying so much to see. Jon came with me to the appointment this time, and I think that really helped because he was able to ask several of his own questions, and I gained some new perspective on the various treatment options.

It took me three and a half years to sit down and have this discussion with my husband, but after seeing the new doctor, that is exactly what Jon and I did. We reasoned through every option, considering the intrinsic value of the life of the embryos created in the IVF procedure and also considering that they were ours. In the end, we came to the same conclusion. We felt comfortable with the ethics of the IVF procedure, but we did not want to go down that road.

The chance of having several extra embryos that would need to be frozen was high. I was already thirty-four, and I didn't want to be coming back and implanting frozen embryos well into my late thirties or early forties. We wanted one or maybe two more kids, not six. Not to mention that I was anxious to get off this emotional roller coaster just as soon as I could. In my heart, I just could not donate the embryos any more than I could give up my own child for adoption. And letting them die was certainly not an option.

Thankfully, this doctor had given us other options to consider. I had already tried artificial insemination with my original OB while taking the pills. But my new doctor suggested that perhaps the more effective shots were a better option for me. Jon and I decided we'd try the shots two times.

I'm often surprised at how many couples are struggling with infertility. I had so much support and encouragement from several friends who had been there before or were going through it with me. It really was a blessing. But three months and over three thousand dollars later, Jon and I got off the emotional roller coaster, spent and with no baby.

So now it was time to move on. Jon and I were able to get away for a nice one-week vacation by ourselves while James stayed with Grandma and Grandpa. We had a great time together hiking, kayaking, and mountain biking. It reminded us of when we were first married. But at the end of the week, we were also reminded of why we chose to have kids in the first place. We had been on a lot of adventures together, but we wanted to share those adventures with someone else. We realized we were not at capacity. We still had more love to give.

When we got home, the desire to have more children continued to grow. The old thoughts that had been plaguing me over the past three years also began to resurface.

If we don't have any more kids, who will take care of James when we are old and gone? James will probably never get married. If we don't have more kids, we will never have grandkids. Jon will never be able to coach his kid's team, or watch her in the play, or teach him how to drive a car.

This and so many other good and healthy things that Jon and I desired prompted us to take another look at IVF. One of my close friends was undergoing the procedure at the time, and she and her husband had decided to limit the number of eggs that they fertilized. That way they didn't run the risk of having six or more frozen babies when they really only wanted one or maybe two more children. Jon and I really liked this idea. It is a financial risk because the fewer embryos you attempt to make the lower your chances of conceiving become. But we decided that the financial risk was far less important than the risk of having so many embryos, so we decided to give it a try.

In October 2008, exactly four years into my infertility journey, I began the series of pills and shots that prompted my body to grow to maturity a large number of eggs. It was terribly uncomfortable having all those eggs in there, and I was anxious to have the short surgery where the doctor removes them. The surgery transpired without incident, and I was sent home with a prescription for Vicodin, should the "mild discomfort" be a problem.

As it turned out, the "uncomfortable" pain I was experiencing before the surgery was nothing compared to the pain that was to follow. It started on the car ride home from the surgery and only got worse. My body had overreacted to all the hormones, and my ovaries were continuing to produce fluid even after my eggs had been extracted.

As the days passed and my embryos began to grow in their tiny test tube, the pain in my abdomen also continued to grow. Over the next five days, my entire belly filled with fluid, putting pressure on all of my internal organs. The night before I was to have my embryos transferred back into my uterus, I decided to see if I could make it through the night without the Vicodin. For obvious reasons, I was highly sensitive to birth defects, and I didn't want to be taking those high-dose pain pills, or any pills for that matter, until at least the vulnerable first trimester was over. I didn't care how safe the doctor said they were. Not that I felt like what happened to James was my fault, but this time around, I wanted no regrets.

I tossed and turned all night, and by about 3:00 a.m., I decided I couldn't take it anymore and asked Jon to fetch me one of the pills. I was in so much pain that I could barely breathe or talk.

"I think maybe you should go to the hospital," said Jon.

"Let's just wait a half hour to give the medicine time to get into my system," I said with short breaths, almost as if I were in labor. By that time, my belly was so large that it did appear that I was about five months pregnant.

Jon sat nervously in bed next to me as we watched the half hour tick off the clock. If the pain medicine made any difference during that time, I couldn't tell. Everything always seems worse in the middle of the night, but all I could think about was my nurse friend telling me that people have died from complications of IVF. Thankfully, my mom was staying with us. The plan was for her to help with James during the bed-rest period required after the embryo transfer. Jon woke her up.

When we got to the ER at 4:30 a.m., it looked like a ghost town. I was so happy that they were able to take me back right away and give me morphine for the pain. The doctor ordered both an external and internal ultrasound.

After another hour wait, the doctor came back with a print out. Pointing to the black-and-white picture, he said, "Your abdomen is filled with large pockets of fluid. It might be blood. Don't eat or drink anything. You'll probably be having surgery within a few hours. This is very dangerous. We need to figure out where this is coming from."

We discussed everything that I'd done for the IVF, and I insisted he talk to my doctor before proceeding. Thankfully, my fertility doctor was just across the street and, by that time, his office was open. After some time, the ER doc returned with a change in tune.

"Your doctor wants you to come to his office right now. You're free to go."

After yet another round of ultrasounds at my doctor's office, they were able to confirm that I had ovarian hyper-stimulation. The large pockets were not blood but only the fluid coming from my ovaries.

"Over time, it should absorb back into your body," he said.

My doctor was able to prescribe some stronger pain medication to help me deal with the recovery, but he highly advised that we freeze the two embryos that had survived the fertilization process and were still growing and healthy. As sick as I was, becoming pregnant was not a healthy choice for me or the embryos. So we placed in cryopreservation the two remaining hopes we had for another child, and I began what would be a full two weeks of painful recovery.

At this point in my life, I am beginning to understand that life is a delicate balance between being content with what God had given and yet always desiring more of the good things He can give. Not that I am actually always content, but I am learning. As I write this chapter, I am about two months away from transplanting our frozen embryos back into my body. I don't know what the outcome will be. It is a good thing to want a child. Children are a gift from the Lord. But just because it is a good thing doesn't mean that God will grant it. It is in His capable hands.

Desire realized is sweet to the soul.

Proverbs 13:19

Hope deferred makes the hart sick, But desire fulfilled is a tree of life.

Proverbs 13:12

As we'll learn in the next few chapters, our *greatest* desire should be for the good things God has waiting for us in heaven. But that doesn't mean we shouldn't desire good things here on earth as well. God doesn't just bless us with trials that help us mature; He blesses us with many happy and rewarding things in this life too.

I have a friend who got married a little later in life than most. For several years, she wondered if she would ever meet the one. Her desire to be married was very strong. And she knew that it was a good desire or at least not an unrighteous one. (While marriage is permitted, it is actually recommended by Paul to remain single so that you might have "undistracted devotion to the Lord"; see 1 Corinthians 7:25-40.) One time, she had someone tell her that because it was a righteous desire to get married, clearly the desire had come from God and He wouldn't give her this strong desire unless He was planning to fulfill it. Well, she wasn't sure if she bought that, and as it turns out, it simply is not true.

King David was a man whose heart was "wholly devoted" to the Lord (1 Kings 11:4). He was a man who "walked, in integrity of heart and uprightness, doing according to all that [God had] commanded…" (1 Kings 9:4). But he was also a man of war. He was king over Israel in a time when her enemies both outside and within were constantly attacking, and as a mighty warrior, David had shed much blood in his defense of God's people and of the kingdom.

"Now it came about when the king lived in his house, and the LORD had given him rest on every side from all his enemies, that the king said to Nathan the prophet, 'See now, I dwell in a house of cedar, but the ark of God dwells within tent curtains'" (2 Samuel 7:1-2). It was David's desire to build a house for God. God replied through Nathan the prophet that David would not build a house but that his son, Solomon, would. And several years later, when Solomon completed the temple, this is what he said:

> Now it was in the heart of my father David to build a house for the name of the LORD, the God of Israel. But the LORD said to my father David, "Because it was in your heart to build a house for My name, *you did well* that it was in your heart. Nevertheless you shall not build the house, but your son who will be born to you, he will build the house for My name."
>
> 1 Kings 8:18-19 (emphasis mine)

David was a godly man, and he had a righteous desire. God said that he did well to have that righteous desire.

Is it okay to have desires for earthly things? Well, it depends on what you desire. Just like your actions and emotions, your desires must be brought under the lordship of Christ. But if they have, embrace them, don't give up hope for them, and earnestly pursue them. Our righteous desires are pleasing to God, even if they go unrealized (1 Kings 8:18), as David's desire to build the temple for God did.

The Bible is full of examples of godly desire. Solomon had a godly desire for intimacy with his wife (Song of Solomon 7:10). Paul had desires to build a close discipleship relationship with several people in his life. Another example of a godly desire is for someone's salvation (Romans 10:1) or for wisdom (Proverbs 3:15) or for your own closer relationship with the Lord. "Christianity has nothing to say to the person who is completely happy with the way things are. Its message is for those who hunger and thirst—for those who desire life as it was meant to be."[15] God has designed us in such a way that we should always feel a certain level of discontentment. For the unbeliever, this discontentment draws them to Christ. For the believer, we live in a constant state of discontentment with the things of this world and a desire for the things of heaven. God has intended us to feel this way (2 Corinthians 5:1-9). For David, his greatest desire was for God Himself. He wrote, "O God... I shall seek You earnestly; My soul thirsts for You, my flesh yearns for You...because Your lovingkindness is better than life...my soul is satisfied..." (Psalm 63:1-5).

At this point, you might be asking: What if I desire that more intimate relationship with my spouse but never get it? What if I am like David, time and time again, and my righteous hopes are deferred? What if my aunt that I love so dearly never comes to a saving faith? Should I really keep on hoping, with my emotions fully in the game, only to be trampled underfoot?

Sometimes when people run into difficulties or pain when they are pursuing righteous desires, they just give up and say, "Maybe it just wasn't meant to be." My favorite response to that is, "Or maybe it was just meant to be hard." Don't give up on something just because it's hard. Take courage. We have no idea what is meant to be. We can never know ahead of time what God's plan is in these matters.

God often gives us incredibly difficult assignments. Do you think it was easy for Abraham to lay his son on that altar? Do you think it was easy for Moses to approach Pharaoh and say, "Let God's people go"? And do you think that Peter looked on the risen Christ for the first time and didn't feel the pain in the depths of his soul for the denial that had taken place only a few days before?

Maybe I am never meant to have another child. But maybe I am and God just wanted me to take this difficult journey to get there. Maybe I had something to learn. Certainly I have learned a lot. If nothing else, this long and drawn-out trial has continued to motivate me to write this book. The bottom line is I will never know if I am meant to have another child until either that child is conceived or my childbearing years have passed and I have no second child. We cannot predict the details of the plans that God has for us. We can only continue to seek good things, hunger, thirst, and earnestly desire God's best for us because our righteous desires please Him.

> I would have despaired unless I had believed that I would see the goodness of the LORD in the land of the living. Wait for the LORD; be strong and let your heart take courage; yes, wait for the LORD.
>
> Psalm 27:13-14

CONSIDER IT ALL JOY WHEN YOU ENCOUNTER VARIOUS TRIALS

James 1:2

One of our favorite getaways is Boone, North Carolina. It is a smaller city nestled in the middle of the Blue Ridge Mountains, about a two-hour drive from our house. As you begin the slow ascent up through the foothills, the highway becomes lined with thick birch groves mixed with towering maples that are breathtaking in the fall. As the mountains in the distance come into view, the landscape breaks from the trees into a series of Christmas tree farms that dot the rolling hills. The final turns leading up to the high country are flanked with some of the oldest mountains in this country. Many people go there to visit the cute shops nearby or root for the Mountaineers of Appalachian State University. But we love all the outdoor activities that are available only miles from town. There is hiking, camping, canoeing, tubing, biking, and skiing in the winter.

One Saturday in the summer of 2006, we took James up there just to tool around for the day. We stopped at the quaint little coffee shop on the outskirts of town and were just sitting down at a table with our precious brew when a man and his wife walked in the door. I only saw him out of the corner of my eye at first, but something familiar made me take a second look. Maybe it was the way he walked, almost hunched over but yet a confident gait. Maybe it was his skinny frame or the flannel shirt he was wearing. He had a fishing hat on, so it was hard to tell at first, but when he turned, it was the big, fuzzy, white beard that gave him away. It was James's neurologist from Duke.

I didn't know how he felt about seeing patients out of the office, and I didn't want to impose on his weekend plans, but in the end, I couldn't help myself and slowly got up and approached him in line. Speaking his name loud enough for him to hear me, I said, "Is that you?"

I could tell I took him completely off guard as he responded, "Uh, yeah."

"You remember my son, James," I said pointing over to the table where James was sitting in his stroller.

Never being one for small talk, he said, "Oh yes. Umm…how has he been doing?"

"He's been doing great!" I said. "Actually, this week marks nine full weeks without a seizure. That is a record for him. I guess the surgery combined with the new medicine is working well for him after all."

"Well, that's good to hear," he said as he glanced over at his wife, who looked to me to be a neatly dressed and rather charming lady. He introduced me and James as a patient, a fact I'm sure she had already concluded by then.

"So what brings you up here to Boone?" I asked.

"We've been building a house here. It's actually almost done. We're just overseeing some final details," he said.

We discussed briefly the real estate opportunities in the small town and then parted ways.

Jon and I left the coffee shop feeling so optimistic about James's seizure-free weeks and the opportunities it would give us to get out and explore that great country. But in the back of my mind, I couldn't help but feel a bit anxious knowing that the doctor who had done so much for James—and the one who I had come to respect—was, no doubt, retiring soon.

As it turned out, James began having seizures again shortly after that meeting, about one every two weeks. He even had another one of those morning seizures where the strange thumping sounds coming from the monitor were what woke me up. After the morning seizure, I decided to give the doctor a call.

"James had another seizure in the early morning," I told him.

"How long did it last?" he said.

"I don't know. I was sleeping when it started. He could have been like that for an hour for all I know," I said, clearly a bit exasperated.

"Yes…I see," he said. "Did the Diastat work to stop it?"

"Yes. It took a bit of time, but it did finally work," I said. "What do you suggest I do about these seizures he's having at night?"

After a little pause, he said, "Well, it's possible for kids to have seizures at night."

"Yeah, but a couple of times now he has had a seizure and stopped breathing," I said. "What if that happens in the middle of the night?"

"Well…I'm not sure what you want me to say to that," he said.

I was frustrated and disappointed but, at the same time, glad that he didn't say anything stupid like, "Oh, that won't happen," because I knew that it could. This man wasn't God, and he wasn't pretending to be. He had given me all the help he could, and that was it.

What can I do to prevent my son from dying in the middle of the night from a seizure? I rolled the question over in my head day after day. I think that deep down inside, I knew the answer to the question. There was nothing I could do. But I still wasn't prepared to fully relinquish control. I decided to purchase a sleep apnea monitor that was intended to prevent SIDS in infants. My husband was quick to point out that the monitor works by detecting motion. And if James is seizing and not breathing, the monitor will not go off. I acknowledged his point. *But at least I'll know it right away if he stops moving*, I thought, *and hopefully it won't be too late.*

As summer became fall, James's seizure frequency began to increase, and by mid-October, the neurologist had suggested we schedule an appointment with the surgeon. One of the side effects of the big surgery James had was that fluid could build up pressure in the open space where his right brain had been removed. If James's brain had built up pressure, then it could be why he was having seizures again. The treatment for the pressure was to place a shunt in his brain, a small tube with a valve that released the fluid down into his abdomen.

As the doctor explained how the device worked, I couldn't help but think back to that first appointment at the high-risk pregnancy specialist. I had cried so much just thinking about the possibility that my unborn child would have to have a shunt. I never even imagined back then the roller coaster that our lives had become over the past three years. And now here we were, back to the original solution. But what it meant was so very different.

There were several tests leading up to it, but by January 5, James was once more scheduled for surgery. This type of surgery was fairly routine, and the risk of complications was much lower. Our family decided to stay home, and Jon and I got to spend some good family bonding time with James before the surgery.

As Jon and I lay in bed the night before the surgery, not too anxious to fall asleep, he said, "I can't believe this is it."

"What do you mean?" I said.

"Well, this is our last option. When James was born, the doctors said that if the medication doesn't work to control his seizures, then the only other realistic treatment options were the hemispherectomy surgery followed by the shunt," he said. "So if this doesn't work, we're out of options."

"Yeah, I suppose you're right, but there are more medicines to try," I said.

"Maybe a few more, but I'm guessing we've probably tried about eighty percent of what's out there. What are the chances that the one or two that we haven't tried will work?" he said.

I was a bit frustrated. My husband has a knack for calling it like it is. My mind didn't want to go there. My entire life I had dealt with problems by either fixing them or just living with them. "Fix it or shut up about it" was my motto. But I just couldn't live with this problem. This was one of those bad things that if I were to put it on my life's scale, no amount of good on the other side could take away the hurt and stress of it. And the idea that we were down to our last option for fixing it didn't sit well with me.

The next day, the surgery went well, and the doctor was able to confirm when he opened up James's head that the pressure was, in fact, very high. The shunt seemed to be working properly, and Jon and I left the hospital once again with optimism and a hope that this might be the end to James's seizures.

But we weren't left to hope for long. In the four weeks after the shunt surgery, James had twenty-five seizures. I probably would have been devastated had I not been distracted by a new development. Just a few days after the surgery, James's skin and certain parts of his body had become very sensitive. He would cry out when I changed his shirt just because the new shirt was cold on his skin.

He still couldn't say many words, so it was hard to tell exactly what was going on, but it seemed like he was having some shoulder and upper leg pain. But the worst was his left arm. He would cradle it in by his belly and wouldn't let anyone touch it. If they did, he would squirm and whine as if in pain. It broke my heart. The surgeon had no explanation. The neurologist didn't have any ideas either.

One particularly hard day for him, I decided to take him to the pediatrician. Even though James could not verbally confirm that he was having pain, they were able to observe the same behavior and made the same conclusion about his pain that I did, but they had no idea why. The doctor even ordered an X-ray of his left arm to rule out a broken bone.

So this is it, I thought as I drove home from the pediatrician. *This is our life now. No more options left to fix the problem. A lifetime of seizures, and who knows what else might happen next.*

Lord, I prayed, *I know I should have joy in these trials, but right now I'm wondering how I'm even going to make it through this life in one piece...*

I thought back through some of the tough times of the past few years and some of the things that I had known my whole life about God but only recently came to really, truly trust. *I know this is no accident. You are still on Your throne. I know this all has a purpose that I can't really see right now. But I can't do this by myself,*

Lord. There were no tears. I had run out of those long ago. I was just being realistic. *I guess from here on, You will have to carry me... like You have so many times before.*

What other option do I have but to hope in Him? I thought. A smile came to my face as I imagined just how great the end would be after such a lifetime as I imagined at that moment I would live. And for the rest of that half-hour ride home, I actually chose joy as I envisioned my faith one day becoming sight and looking my Savior in the eyes as He welcomed me home.

Five weeks after the shunt surgery, my mom asked me to write an update for all the women she knew who were praying for James. I went to write and actually sat amazed that he hadn't had any seizures that week. I also noticed that his sensitivity had started to go down just a bit. I wrote:

> Jon and I really love the spectacular views and the sense of awe that you get from standing on a mountaintop, so for us, making it to the top is worth the difficult climb to get there. Starting the day after his surgery, James had twenty-five seizures over a period of four weeks. He also had a lot of pain, sometimes in very strange places... Just a week ago, we decided to make an increase in one of his medicines, and he has been seizure free since then. Please pray that this increase will continue to work for him for a long time. His sensitivity has gone down just this week too. He did not do much walking or any exercise in January, so he has digressed quite a bit in his walking skills. It seems like he is where he was about six months ago. So we are working hard this month to get him back to his pre-surgery strength. Please pray that it doesn't take as long as it did the first time.
>
> So while things have improved just this week, you might be thinking, *That doesn't sound like a mountaintop to me.* Well,

it's not. It's really only a slight rise in the trail. But off in the distance, we can see just a glimpse of what lies ahead when we do get to the top, even though it is still around the bend, up the cliff, and a lot of sweat and tears along the way. And someday, when we are home with the Lord, the view from that mountain will be way beyond what we can ever hope or imagine. And this present suffering will not be worthy to even compare.

Consider it all joy, my brethren, when you encounter various trials, knowing that the testing of your faith produces endurance. And let endurance have its perfect result, so that you may be perfect and complete, lacking in nothing.

James 1:2-4

So far, we've learned that everyone has trials and that it's okay to be broken and weep over them. We've learned from scripture that we can build our endurance through trials, especially by remembering our faith in God's promises. God's Word tells us that some of those promises for us are that God is in control, God loves us, and that in everything, God has a purpose or a plan, even in our trials. For those who love Him, God is working everything together for our greatest good, and we can trust Him.

We've learned that some of that good could be discipline that takes the form of a trial. We've learned about the importance of prayer during trials and even why God might be silent and therefore seem distant (even though He is never far from us). We've discussed one of the sinful behaviors that can creep up as the result of a trial: coveting. All of these things can help us make it through or persevere, and if we choose to, maybe we can even learn something along the way. But now, in the book of James,

God has raised the bar even higher. He doesn't just want us to make it through. He actually wants us to have joy. Is that really what He's saying? Let's take a closer look.

The word used in this passage that has been translated as *joy* is the Greek word transliterated as "chara."[16] It can also be translated as "gladness." It does not mean some type of inner peace or spiritual contentment but real happiness. Webster defines *joy* as "the emotion evoked by well-being, or by the prospect of possessing what one desires."[17] It seems as if the key to joy is what you desire. We'll come back to this.

The Greek word in the verse translated as *all* is a corporate word. It is used here not in a sense of there being a bunch of different type of joys; rather, it is used to intensify the word. It is as if James is saying, "Consider it super joy or mega joy or great joy."[18]

In the chapter on faith, we talked about the Greek word for *trial* meaning "an experiment" or "the trial of one's fidelity, integrity, virtue, or constancy."[19] It is a general word used throughout the Bible referring to several different types of temptations, trials, or adversities. It is used by Paul in Galatians 4:14 when he talks of his "bodily illness." It is used in Hebrews 3:8 to describe the Hebrew people's plight of wandering in the wilderness for forty years.

The word translated as *consider* in this verse means "to have authority over, to lead."[20] In this case, you are leading yourself. It is a word derived from a word that means to lead an animal. And it has a timeless sense to it, meaning it is like a habit, done over and over.

So putting all this together, it is as if James 1:2 says, "Keep on considering or taking authority over or leading yourself into great joy or super gladness when you encounter all different types of trials..." So yes, God really does want us to be happy when we're faced with a trial. And this joy in trials is clearly a choice. Like all emotions, you have a choice. You can just let emotions happen to you or you can take control of them and thus bring them under the authority of what God wants for your life. You can choose to be angry or not. You can choose to love or not. You can choose to be sad or not. And in this case, you can choose to have joy or not, and God is saying He wants you to choose joy. Of course, all of these things are much easier said than done. So how do we choose to have joy over something that so naturally does not produce joy in us?

One key is found right in James 1:2. He writes, "*Knowing* that the testing of your faith produces endurance..." (emphasis mine). We've already learned that trials test your faith and thereby produce endurance. But then James goes on to write, "And let endurance have its perfect result, so that you may be perfect and complete, lacking nothing" (James 1:4). James is saying that you need to *know* that your trials are producing endurance and that the endurance is perfecting you.

The word translated as *perfect* here means "brought to its end, finished, wanting nothing necessary to completeness, full grown, mature." How many of you feel perfect, full grown, and completely mature? When will our maturity want "nothing necessary to completeness"?

Later in chapter 1, James writes, "Blessed is a man who perseveres under trial; for once he has been approved, he will receive the crown of life which the Lord has promised to those who love Him" (James 1:12).

When do we receive the crown of life? When are we approved? This verse isn't talking about any type of earthly benefit or a benefit to our flesh. The result of faith endurance is your perfection and a crown of life. You need to *know* that if you are among the brethren, these trials are perfecting you and producing for you a reward in heaven.

Remember, joy is the "emotion evoked by the prospect of possessing what one desires." So the bottom line is this: What is your greatest desire? Do you desire the best of what this world has to offer, or do you desire the best of what heaven has to offer? I think if we were honest, we would probably answer both. But consider what Jesus said about seeking the best of what the world can offer:

> Do not store up for yourselves treasures on earth, where moth and rust destroy, and where thieves break in and steal. But store up for yourselves treasures in heaven, where neither moth nor rust destroys, and where thieves do not break in or steal; for where your treasure is, there your heart will be also...No one can serve two masters; for either he will hate the one and love the other, or he will be devoted to one and despise the other. You cannot serve God and wealth.
>
> Matthew 6:19-21, 24

In this case, Jesus was talking about storing up money. But it can also apply to other worldly things, like seeking a trial-free life. If you are eagerly seeking this, you will have very limited success with joy in your trials. Your heart cannot reside in two places.

I have a friend whose mother is a follower of Jesus and had decided to get married for the fifth time, even though it clearly says in God's Word that God hates divorce (Malachi 2:16) and it is adultery to get remarried (Matthew 19:9). Her reasoning was, "God just wants me to be happy." This line of reasoning has never sat well with me. For a long time, I thought that it was not true—God doesn't *always* want you to be happy. But after studying this passage in James, I realized that God does want us to be happy. It's just that He wants us to choose to be happy with *His* will for our life, not *our* will. God's will can clearly be found in His written Word. He doesn't want us to obey as we drag our feet and mutter complaints under our breath. "For this is the love of God, that we keep His commandments; and His commandments are not burdensome" (1 John 5:3b). He wants us to choose to obey Him and be happy with the choice, knowing that His will is going to turn out to be our greatest good and produce for us a reward in heaven.

> We have to learn to obey God's law... If we do not want our hand to be burned, we should not put it in the fire... Submission to God's law is better than many prayers. A minute of revelation of God's way is better than an incessant, ignorant pleading for God's blessings and His help in our works... We often long for blessing but do not even find mercy... We have to learn to humble ourselves under His hand and obey this law. With obedience there is blessing.[21]

It could be that your trial is the direct result of not being obedient to God's will. And as we know from Galatians, when we have sin in our life, we will reap what we sow. But even if you cannot point to any specific sin causing your trial, you still need to realize that these difficult times are part of God's will for your life.

There are so many great blessings God gives us in life where it is easy to choose to be happy and give praise and thanksgiving to God. But as Job said to his wife, "Shall we indeed accept good from God and not accept adversity?" (Job 2:10). We need to learn to trust Him, realizing that sometimes God's will for our lives involves a difficult trial. It will be much easier to choose joy in our trials if we can realize that the trial is part of God's perfect will for our lives. So many times we pray for blessings from God, never realizing that our trial *could be* the answer to that prayer.

As difficult as choosing joy in the midst of our trial can be, it appears that the real challenge is not our circumstances but our perspective. If the key to joy is possessing what we desire and our greatest desire is God's best for us, then it will be much easier to lead ourselves into happiness during our trial knowing that the trial is part of God's will for our life. It helps us know that we are on the right trail and that the trail leads to the ultimate joy in heaven and that the trials we are experiencing along the way are perfecting us and earning for us a great reward when we get there.

After James's twenty-five seizures following his shunt surgery, the doctor decided to increase his new medicine a couple more times. For the last increase, I actually had to get a special note from the doctor before our prescription insurance would cover it because the dose was higher than the recommended treatment dose for that particular medicine. But once his body adjusted to the new dose, he went an incredible eleven months and one week completely seizure free.

After so many disappointments, it was hard for us to believe at first that the seizures were controlled with this new medication. Every time James would make a strange noise or movement, I would stop everything and focus intently on him to make sure he wasn't starting into a seizure. It was hard to let him out of my sight for even a minute for fear that he would start seizing and I would miss it, delaying the administration of his emergency medicine. But as the weeks turned into months, this became much easier.

It wasn't until the following winter, when he had a high fever due to some type of seasonal illness, that he had a few more seizures. And the year after that, he had one when he came down with strep throat. But other than that, he's been completely seizure free.

Even as I write this now, it's hard for me to believe that the frequent seizure part of his life could be behind us. I know that he will always have the diagnosis of epilepsy and when he gets sick the seizures will always be a threat. And even to this day, every single night, when I kneel by his bedside to pray, I ask God, *Please protect him from seizures tonight as he sleeps.*

It's also hard to believe how much my thinking has changed over these years, how much I've learned and grown. I think back to that prideful and self-reliant girl, and I'm actually afraid of the pit of self-destruction I would have been living in had it not been for these trials. I certainly would have never signed up for such a thing, and I don't wish it on anyone. But I see that in my life, given my stubborn personality, there are things that I've learned about myself and about God that I could not have learned any other way. So when I pray every night, I also thank God. I thank Him for giving us James. I thank Him for making my footsteps firm. I thank Him for the work He's done in our lives. I thank Him for the work He's done in James's life. And I rejoice—I rejoice that God didn't give up on me but instead loved me so much to use this experience to test my faith and build my eternal rewards. I rejoice that I've learned a new song. And I rejoice that James, at least for that day, was seizure free.

I waited patiently for the LORD; and He inclined to me and heard my cry. He brought me up out of the pit of destruction, out of the miry clay, and He set my feet upon a rock making my footsteps firm. He put a new song in my mouth, a song of praise to our God; Many will see and fear and will trust in the LORD.

Psalm 40:1-3

I GO TO PREPARE A PLACE FOR YOU

John 14:2

It was shortly before James's third birthday when I decided to go visit the public school in our county that was dedicated specifically for kids with special needs. It's rare that the public school system would even have such a thing, but from all I heard, this place had a very good reputation. In fact, it was rumored that people from all over the state and even country would move into our county just to be able to attend the school. If you qualify for special ED, then you can begin school at age three instead of five, and James's third birthday was only a few months away.

It seemed like a great opportunity for him. James has always been a social little guy, probably more social than his dad and I put together. He loves being out and about and meeting new people. All of the therapies that he had been getting at home would now be at the school. Plus, I was thinking about doing more contract mechanical engineering work, so the thought of not having to pay for childcare was appealing too.

Despite all the positives, something was holding me back from sending him there. No doubt I'd miss being with him all day, but it was more than that. When James was born, I knew in my head that he would always carry the new, socially acceptable label of "a special needs child." But then we brought him home and he was just a baby. No other babies could walk or talk. It didn't matter that he wasn't potty trained because all babies wear diapers. He just didn't look that different on the outside.

But he was getting older, and people were starting to notice those differences, even if in my head he was still my little baby boy. Taking him to this school meant accepting a label. It was such a big step for me because it was a clear indicator that nothing miraculous had happened with his development. And just as the doctors had told me, my son was disabled. He was one of "those" kids.

As I headed down the highway that day for our first visit, my mind was whirling. *What will the other kids at the school be like? Will the teachers and staff be nice, or will they be kind of weird? I mean, what type of person works in a place like that anyway? What questions should I ask when I get there? How will I know if it's the right place for James?*

The school visit went okay, and I reluctantly enrolled James to attend starting the following school year.

During that first year, I would drive James to school each morning, and then he would ride the bus home. That way I could ask more detailed questions about the activities he was participating in, ask how he was doing in them, and get to know his teacher better. He still wasn't walking very well, but if you held both his hands, he would slowly cover the terrain. I would walk with him in this way from the car to his classroom each morning, for both the exercise and the practice. Besides, he was starting to get too heavy to carry. One day, only a week or two after school started, I noticed that instead of me directing him, he was leading the way. He actually knew which way to go and which turns to make to navigate the hallways and get to his classroom.

It also seemed to me that he really enjoyed going to school. They had art class, music class (which he really loved), and all sorts of unique activities and assemblies. He had his own special chair at the table in his classroom where they did circle time each morning and were introduced to all sorts of new textures and concepts. After observing for several weeks, it was clear to me that, had James stayed at home, I simply couldn't compete with all that entertainment and input.

Another thing I noticed walking through the halls each morning was that James seemed to be making friends with all of the staff and students. Every adult we passed knew his name and would give him a warm greeting or simply say, "Hey, DeLine!" He got so excited every time someone would talk to him in the halls. One day we saw one of the moms from James's class holding her son's hand and walking in a similar manner. When both boys saw each other, they stopped in their tracks. Neither one of them could talk, but they just stood there looking at each other. One of them reached out to touch the other's arm, and it was almost as if they were having a silent conversation. After a time, they were content to move on. It was so cute.

One day I dropped James off, and his teacher said, "Do you mind if we try putting James on the potty today?"

"Well, no. I guess not. I mean, go for it," I said, thinking in my mind, *Yeah. Good luck, lady.*

That evening, when James got off the bus, I was anxious to read what the teacher had written in his folder. I couldn't believe it. James had actually gone on the potty for the first time. I loved this new teacher. She was sweet yet firm and always had such high expectations for all the kids. She didn't let them get away with much and was always giving them the individualized challenges they needed to bring out the potential in each one. The assistant in the room was more like a sweet grandmother, and I'm sure an hour didn't go by without each one of those kids getting a big hug.

In fact, all of the therapists and various staff were so sweet, and the programs all ran so smoothly. The principle ran a tight ship. You could tell. In an atmosphere where the kids themselves could be so chaotic, order was exactly what they needed. The school was always so clean and uncluttered. And I never saw anyone lose their patience with a child or be discouraging to them in any way. Later I learned that the average number of years that a teacher had been there was sixteen years.

As it turned out, at that point in James's life, there couldn't have been a better place for him to be.

Do not let your heart be troubled; believe in God, believe also in Me. In My Father's house are many dwelling places; if it were not so, I would have told you; for I go to prepare a place for you. If I go and prepare a place for you, I will come again and receive you to Myself, that where I am, there you may be also.

John 14:1-3

After Jesus was raised from the dead, He was taken up into heaven (Acts 1:9). One reason He left was so that He could go prepare a place specifically for each believer. He is preparing a special place, with all the love and care that only a parent could give their child, specifically for you.

What are you looking forward to the most about heaven?

Did you have to think about it for a second? The truth is most of us do not spend a lot of time pondering what heaven will be like or what great rewards will await us when we get there. But Paul says in Colossians 3:1b-2, "Keep seeking the things above, where Christ is…set your mind on the things above, not on the things that are on earth."

It can be very rewarding to be a follower of Jesus in this life. But in reality, atheists, secularists, humanists, and followers of other religions all have ways to be rewarded in this life. If there were no promise of heaven and no promise of a future resurrection from the dead, then this Christianity thing just isn't worth it. As Paul said in 1 Corinthians 15:19, "If we have hoped in Christ in this life only, we are of all men most to be pitied."

The book *Mistaken Identity* tells the true story of two college-aged girls who were in the same terrible car accident. The girls were both followers of Jesus. One lived and the other did not. But there was a mistake at the accident scene and the girls' identities were switched. The father who thought his daughter was in heaven writes this in the book:

> "What is her new home like? I've always known where Whitney was, and when something great happened to her, she would come home bubbling over and tell me about it. I wonder what she wants to tell me now about all the great things that have happened since she arrived in heaven?"
>
> The more Newell thought about Whitney's new home, the more anxious he became to discover the answers… Over the next several weeks he read several books about heaven… The more he read, the more real the place became, and the more anxious he became to go there and join his daughter, singing praises to God.[22]

This awful trial in this father's life turned out to focus his thoughts more toward heaven. In James chapter one, we learned that our trials are perfecting us and earning for us a great reward in heaven. But what exactly will heaven be like? Will it really be worth it when we get there?

The truth is we don't know a lot about what heaven is like. Jesus spoke of the promise of it often, but not a lot about the particulars of what it would be like. But we do know some things.

First, we know that what we do here on earth has a direct bearing on how we live there. In 1 Corinthians 3, Paul writes, "But each will receive his own reward according to his own labor" (verse 8). He goes on to compare us to master builders who are constructing on a foundation in Jesus Christ. Some build with wood, hay, and straw, while others build with gold, silver, and precious stones. "Each man's work will become evident; for the day will show it because it is to be revealed with fire, and the fire itself will test the quality of each man's work. If any man's work which he has built on it remains, he will receive a reward" (1 Corinthians 3:13-14).

We know that heaven is a place where we will be with Jesus. When Jesus left to prepare a place for us, He said He would return to "receive you to Myself, that where I am, there you may be also" (John 14:3). When Jesus was on the earth, one of His ultimate desires was for us to be in heaven with Him. In John 17:24a, He was praying shortly before His death, and He said, "Father, I desire that they also, whom You have given Me, be with Me where I am..."

The thought of seeing my Savior face-to-face, to have all my faith suddenly become sight, to learn more about God, and to have so many of my questions answered are some of the things that make heaven exciting to me. But more than our own unique expectations, we have this promise: "You will make known to me the path of life; in Your presence is fullness of joy; in Your right hand there are pleasures forever" (Psalm 16:11).

When we receive Jesus as our Savior, we become not mere servants or slaves but actually adopted children of God (Romans 8:15-17). And our promise of heaven is our inheritance. Listen to how Peter describes our inheritance:

> Blessed be the God and Father of our Lord Jesus Christ, who according to His great mercy has caused us to be born again to a living hope through the resurrection of Jesus Christ from the dead, to obtain an inheritance which is imperishable and undefiled and will not fade away, reserved in heaven for you, who are protected by the power of God through faith for a salvation ready to be revealed in the last time. In this you greatly rejoice, even though now for a little while, if necessary, you have been distressed by various trials, so that the proof of your faith, being more precious than gold which is perishable, even though tested by fire, may be found to result in praise and glory and honor at the revelation of Jesus Christ.
>
> 1 Peter 1:3-7

Our inheritance is imperishable and undefiled. And similar to what was taught in James, the distress of our various trials is proving our faith. And the proving of that faith is earning us a reward. And here, Peter says that the reward is more precious than gold and when Jesus comes it will "be found to result in praise and glory and honor."

Sometimes we can get so caught up with what looks to be good to us in this perishable and defiled world that we don't even strive for a higher goal. My nephew came to visit us when he was just nine years old. My husband took him for a tour of the gas pump factory where he worked. They went into the office, and he showed him the marketing department and the engineering stations. He explained the president's role and the other jobs like accounting and sales. Then they went out to the hot and dirty factory to look at all the machines creating parts for the gas pumps. Finally, they stopped in front of a loud and oily machine that was stamping out little metal pieces as a man guided the metal strip into the slot. My husband then asked my nephew, "So which job to you think you want to have when you grow up?"

My nephew paused for a bit and looked around the factory. His eyes finally rested on the loud machine directly in front of them pounding out the shiny little metal pieces and said, "I guess I'd like to do that job."

You see, his nine-year-old mind couldn't fully understand what it was like to be an engineer or a president. He didn't understand the long-term implications of sitting in front of that machine day in and day out. He just saw something shiny and loud in front of him and decided, "Yeah, I guess I'll take that."

In a similar way, we can be guilty of seeing the best of what the world has to offer and striving only for that. Just because our mortal minds can't fully comprehend what heaven will be like doesn't mean we should stop short of wanting the best of what God has to offer us there.

Richard Wurmbrand, founder of Voice of the Martyrs, in his book, *The Answer to the Atheist's Handbook*, describes it this way.

> Men are like frogs living at the bottom of some dark well, from which they can see nothing from the outside world. Believers are like men who, while living in such conditions, have heard the singing of a skylark. And miracle of miracles—they have understood the song! It speaks about sun and moon and stars and tree-covered mountains and hills and a wonderful sea. They have faith in this song. They have the assurance that there exists a heavenly paradise. Without neglecting their

earthly duties, they strive toward this heavenly paradise and call others to join them.[23]

God has given us so many opportunities to increase our rewards in heaven, many coming in the form of trials. Let's not have our greatest desire be only what good things this life has to offer, which don't amount to more than pounding out little parts in a gas pump factory. Instead, let us strive for the unknown, trusting God that His reward will be far better than we can ever hope for or imagine.

MOMENTARY LIGHT
AFFLICTION

2 Corinthians 4:17

I could feel people eyeballing me as they walked into the grocery store. Perhaps they were thinking that they should stop and help, but they didn't really know how. Maybe they were thinking, *Why is that lady trying to stuff her five year-old-son into the front of that grocery cart? Can't she see he's just too big for that little seat now?*

James screamed loudly at me as I tried to twist his ankle braces at just the right angle to get them to slide into those vertical holes, just bringing more attention to our struggle. He was so heavy, and for some reason, he wasn't cooperating at all. With one final shove, I was finally successful, and James was now seated in the front of the cart. The bar that went between his legs *did* look uncomfortable.

Poor guy. I'm glad he has a diaper on, I thought as I tried to adjust his bottom on the seat to give him a little more room up front.

Putting both hands on my lower back and giving it a little rub, I stretched back as far as I could. It had been a hard week. James was off school on spring break, so he had been home with me every day. I enjoyed playing and spending the time with him, but all the lifting and bending was finally taking a toll on my back.

He had been using the potty rather inconsistently for over a year now, which was great. But it also meant that I had to carry him there, get his pants down while bending over, and lift him up onto the seat. He was still walking okay if you held both his hands, but he wasn't tall enough yet to keep you from bending down in the process. I tried to walk with him as much as I could, but it was almost easier on my back (and certainly faster) to just carry him. I played a lot of sports and had many injuries as a young girl, so I've always struggled with back and hip pain, even before James came along.

As James and I made our way through the store, it was easy to forget the struggle to get him into the cart. Even to this day, James is a big-time hugger, and for some reason, he gives even twice as many hugs at the grocery store. We were averaging about two big bear hugs per aisle as we grabbed our eggs and headed for the checkout line.

But then it came time to load all that stuff in the car, and I was once more struggling with how to get James out of that cart and into his car seat without turning his legs into a tangled mess. By the time I was successful, my back was telling me I'd better not attempt to lift another thing.

As I drove the short distance home, I sighed, thinking, *I guess I shouldn't be taking him to the grocery store by myself any more. He's just getting too big.*

That year in school, he had made some good progress and could sign about fifty words now. James is almost always in a great mood. He's such a happy little guy and almost never complains. As we drove into the garage, I could see in the mirror that he was getting really excited and was signing, *outside.*

I said, "Yes, James, we're outside."

But he said, "Uh-uh," (his version of *no*) and pointed to his scooter sitting just outside his window in the garage while signing, *outside*, several more times. For his birthday the year before, we had gotten him a Harley-Davidson scooter. It had two wheels in the back, making it more stable, and a headlight that actually lit up in the front, and the handle bars had a pretend throttle that made a great motorcycle sound when you turned it. I would stand him up on it, holding my hands over his, and push him around in the driveway. He loved it. But it was a pretty good workout for me and quite punishing on my back.

It was a nice day out, and I noticed as we drove in that a lot of the other kids in the neighborhood were out in their yards, riding bikes, running after balls and trucks, and playing in the dirt, just like little kids James's age like to do.

I felt so terrible. My little boy just wanted to go out and play like all the other kids. There were many days that I could help him do that. But that day I just couldn't, and I knew he really didn't understand why.

"No, James, we can't play outside today," I said, putting my forehead down on the steering wheel of the car as tears began to well up in my eyes.

I sat there for a time, realizing that the bigger James got, the less I'd be able to help him do normal things. He was starting to become aware of what he wanted and didn't want, and he was learning how to express it. He was even starting, I think, to become aware that he was different. And I was becoming aware of just how limited I was in my ability to help him with that. James was going to have to learn, just as Jon and I had, that "In this life, you will have trouble."

In Romans 7 and 8, Paul described a battle that we enter into when we become a follower of Jesus Christ. When we accept Jesus as our Savior, our inner man is made alive. It is our inner man that is made righteous and wants to serve and please God. As believers, we have made up our minds that we want to serve God. But at the same time, our outer man or our flesh/sin nature remains and is in a constant battle with our inner man or new self. Paul says, "So then, on the one hand I myself with my mind am serving the law of God, but on the other, with my flesh the law of sin" (Romans 7:25b).

So the daily battle we have is to say "no" to the old self and "yes" to the new self. As Paul says, "In reference to your former manner of life, you lay aside the old self, which is being corrupted in accordance with the lusts of deceit…and put on the new self, which in the likeness of God has been created in righteousness and holiness of the truth" (Ephesians 4:22, 24).

Trials are usually outward/worldly things, and God uses outward things to chip away or remove our ugly outer man. Trials help us "lay aside the old self."

It is our flesh/sin nature, or our outer man, that finds issues with our trials. Our inner man, which has been made alive in Christ, is able to find joy in them as the book of James described, but our outer man wants to seek the trial-free life that the world promotes. As Watchman Nee put it, "We have to remember that all misunderstandings, complaints, and dissatisfactions arise from only one thing—secret self love. Because we love ourselves [our old self/flesh] secretly, we try to save ourselves."[24]

Jesus, after talking about His own death, said to those listening, "If anyone wished to come after Me, he must deny himself, and take up his cross daily and follow Me. For whoever wishes to save his life will lose it, but whoever loses his life for My sake, he is the one who will save it" (Luke 9:23-24). Jesus was talking about our old self. If we want to follow Him, we need to deny our old self with its self-centered wants and pleasures. In fact, Paul said in Philippians 3, "I count all things to be loss in view of the surpassing value of knowing Christ Jesus my Lord… that I may know Him and the power of His resurrection and the fellowship of His sufferings, being conformed to His death" (Philippians 3:8-10). Our old self actually needs to die; it needs to be "conformed to His death." In 2 Corinthians 4, Paul says we are "always carrying about in the body the dying of Jesus, so that the life of Jesus also may be manifested in our body."

In other words, this life is a refining fire. We are carrying around a dying body. We are to put no confidence in the flesh (Philippians 3:3) because our flesh is decaying (2 Corinthians 4:16). And with every trial, it is getting beat down and damaged and just getting uglier as it dies.

But there is a reason God wants our flesh dead: "so that the life of Jesus also may be manifested in our body." Do you want to be used by God? Do you want to bear fruit (John 12:24) and be useful for Him? Do you want His life to actually manifest in you? If so, your outer man must die.

"When our outer man is smitten, dealt with, and humbled by all kinds of misfortune, the scars and wounds that are left behind will be the very places from which the spirit flows out from within."[25]

Meanwhile, as we endure our trials, our inner man, which has already been made alive by Jesus, is being "renewed day by day" (2 Corinthians 4:16). Our new self is getting stronger and purer and more beautiful with each trial as our faith is gaining endurance, and we are made more perfect.

And one day, the rottenness of our flesh just won't be able to hang on anymore, and it's just going to fall away. We will enter heaven, where "the sufferings of this present time are not worthy to be compared with the glory that is to be revealed to us" (Romans 8:18).

Jesus is our example "who for the joy set before Him endured the cross, despising the shame, and has sat down at the right hand of the throne of God. For consider Him who has endured such hostility by sinners against Himself, so that you will not grow weary and lose heart" (Hebrews 12:2b-3).

We do not suffer without purpose. Just like Jesus's death brought life to so many, so our sufferings can minister to others (2 Corinthians 1:5-6). And after Christ suffered and died, He was glorified (Philippians 2:8-9). In a similar way, we will face suffering here in this life. And when we go on to live with Jesus, we too will be transformed, conformed to His glory (Philippians 3:20-21). In fact, Paul says that God is preparing us for this very purpose (2 Corinthians 5:5) to be glorified in heaven with Him.

> We are afflicted in every way, but not crushed; perplexed, but not despairing; persecuted, but not forsaken; struck down, but not destroyed; always carrying about in the body the dying of Jesus, so that the life of Jesus also may be manifested in our body...knowing that He who raised the Lord Jesus will raise us also with Jesus and will present us with you... Therefore we do not lose heart, but though our outer man is decaying, yet our inner man is being renewed day by day. For momentary, light affliction is producing for us an eternal weight of glory far beyond all comparison, while we look not at the things which are seen, but at the things which are not seen; for the things which are seen are temporal, but the things which are not seen are eternal.
>
> 2 Corinthians 4:8-10, 14, 16-18

WHO DO YOU SAY
THAT I AM?

Matthew 16:15

Beep, beep, beep, beep, beep…

I reached up and pressed the silent button on the IV pump. I didn't want the sound to disturb James. I pressed the nurse call button on the side of the bed, and a voice that was, I thought, much louder than it needed to be for 11:00 at night came from the speaker.

"May I help you?"

"Yes. My son's IV is beeping again."

It wasn't long before the nurse appeared in the room to make the necessary adjustments to keep the machine quiet for maybe another hour or so. I settled back in next to James on the bed. He still felt so cold. I pulled him closer and tucked the blankets in around us. He had been lethargic before he went to sleep. Very quiet, hardly responding at all. My happy, content little boy seemed to be fading away. His core was still warm, but his arms and legs were very cool to the touch. I shut my eyes as the tears began to well up. I felt like I was losing him. I began to pray silently, but I could really only think of one thing to ask.

Lord, please don't take him from me. Not now. Not yet. Please, please, please, God. Please don't take him from me.

My mind drifted from my prayer as I felt the little movements in my belly. I thought back to the joyful news we had received just five days before. The IVF had been successful, and we were expecting twins, a little boy and a little girl. The ultrasound showed that they both seemed to be growing healthy, with normal brain anatomy. I had not felt too much movement from the babies up until then, so it was just the calming reassurance I needed to allow my exhausted body to drift off to sleep.

The previous week, just a few weeks before his sixth birthday, James had battled strep throat and perhaps a stomach bug and was throwing up through the night. The pediatrician had given him an antibiotic, and he seemed to perk up right away, eating and especially drinking much better. Then later that afternoon, he had a seizure. It was the first seizure he'd had in over a year. I theorized that it was probably because I had given him too much to drink. He was no doubt dehydrated because of all the vomiting. And then, that afternoon, he drank three full cups of water. His little body just couldn't handle that big of a change that quickly.

A few days later, all signs of the infection were gone. However, he still wasn't acting like himself. Monday morning, I called the pediatric neurologist on-call at Duke, and she suggested we check James's sodium level. One of his seizure medications had a side effect of low sodium. I returned to the pediatrician that morning, and they drew his blood.

While I waited for the results, I thought I would go ahead and take James to school. He had been out for over a week due to the illness, and I thought perhaps he just needed to get back into a routine and he'd start feeling and acting more like himself. I had just returned from the school and put my feet up in my favorite chair when the pediatrician called.

"How's James doing?" he said.

"Uhh. The same," I said.

The doctor's voice sounded concerned, and for some reason, I didn't want to let on that I had just dropped him off at school.

"His sodium is a hundred and six. Normal range is one thirty-five to one forty-five."

"Oh, that *is* low," I replied, having no idea how low it really was or just how serious low sodium could be. "So should I give him some Gatorade?"

"Actually, he's going to have to have an IV to get his level back up. I've arranged for you to take him to the hospital. The level needs to be brought up very slowly to avoid other complications in the brain. I would plan on staying a day or two," he said.

I jumped to my feet and packed a bag for two nights, grabbed some of James's favorite videos, and headed out the door to his school.

So there we were in the hospital, almost two days later, and James's sodium levels were not improving. They were drawing his blood every two hours to test the level. It had started to creep up to around 110, but every time a gain was made, he took a step back a few hours later. The sodium they were giving him with the IV appeared to be going right through him. It was a fitful second night's sleep for me as I tossed and turned on that little chair/bed in James's room, trying to get comfortable with my growing belly. The next morning, James seemed to be equally exhausted.

Our local hospital didn't have a pediatric neurologist, so I called his doctor at Duke. He returned my call later that morning, and after our short discussion, the conclusion seemed obvious. James needed to be at Duke, where they had all of his records and more specialized care. By that afternoon, the ambulance crew had arrived to transport him.

James really enjoyed his ride in the big truck. He was so weak from being sick and so mad at being poked and prodded. It was the first time I remember him being happy in more than a week, which was very abnormal for him. When we arrived at Duke, they admitted him to the pediatric intensive care unit. They put him in the same room that he was in when he came out of his hemispherectomy surgery four years earlier. I remembered it like it was yesterday.

After we arrived, I tried to explain to the Duke doctors in detail all the things that had been attempted at the other hospital, but they seemed determined to start from scratch and do basically the same things that the others had done. So we sat in the PICU for another two days with really no improvement. It was during that time that I met the pediatric nephrologist, the kidney specialist. I had no idea what nephrology even was, let alone that James would end up needing prolonged care from one. I learned that the pituitary gland sends a message to your brain, which then sends a message to your kidneys telling them the proper amount of sodium to maintain in your body.

The nephrologist was an average-looking man, maybe in his early fifties, with a thick brown mustache. He was the head of the department. The first time I remember seeing him, he didn't say a word. He came to James's bed side and stood there for quite some time, reading all the fluid bags on his IV pole. He gave me a quick glance and walked out of the room. I had met so many different doctors by then that I had to ask the nurse which one he was after he left. No one had given us any answers or anything even close to a cause for all this, but I thought this guy might be our best hope.

"Oh no," I said to the nurse. "That was the doctor I wanted to talk to. Do you think he'll come back?"

"I don't know. Sometimes they do, and sometimes they don't," she said.

A doctor—I assume it was the nephrologist—decided to increase the concentration of the sodium going into James's IV and continue the diet restriction. The doctors at our local hospital had given orders that James couldn't eat or drink anything. It had already been a couple days of that, and with how sick he had been the week before, poor James had already lost almost four pounds. My hope was that he could begin to eat again soon, but they decided he must wait. After another day or two, his levels did start to increase slightly, but not nearly in proportion to what they were giving him.

The mustached doctor appeared again. This time, after once more doing a thorough examination of the IV bags, he did a short physical exam of James. I noticed he was wearing hearing aids and had to take them out to use his stethoscope. It was interesting to me that in such a cutthroat and demanding field, something that might be looked at by his peers as a weakness had not held this man back, and now here he was, the head of his department at a very prestigious hospital. I thought better of him for it. So I guess that is why I wasn't too bothered when he asked me if I had been sneaking James anything to drink.

A courteous, "No," was all I answered, but I wanted to say, "*Are you kidding?*"

It had been such a hard few days for James. He couldn't say more than maybe a dozen words, but *eat* was one of them. He also knew the sign for *drink*. Over and over again, about every twenty minutes, James would make his request: *Mama, eat.* It broke my heart. He had no idea why he was in the hospital, let alone why he suddenly couldn't eat. I spent those days putting some Vaseline on his lips to keep them from being cracked and dry. It was all I could do to not sneak him something. But by then I understood how serious low sodium could be, and the fact that James was not really improving only fueled my will to say, "No."

It's a strange thing being in the hospital for an extended period of time. The constant hum and beeping of machines and monitors from all around tends to contribute to a monotony that makes you lose track of time. It's never quite light enough, but it never really gets dark at night either, and the days pass by almost unnoticed. Someone is always coming around to take a temperature or check an IV. You never get any privacy, yet still you seem all alone. You're never really busy, but you never have enough free time to even sit and read a book. The world tends to shrink down to the one room you're occupying and the view you get down the hall. In some ways, it is almost relaxing because you leave all the other worries of your life behind and tend to be singularly focused. No bills to pay, no laundry or dishes to do, no schedule to keep.

So I was amazed at how quickly seven days had gone by when the nurse came in and told me they were moving James out of the PICU and onto the main floor. The increased concentration of sodium in his IV, combined perhaps with the medicine change had allowed James's level to creep up to 129. It had taken much longer than anyone could have predicted, but he seemed to be on the mend. And even better, James had been allowed to eat something the past few days, and as they were moving him to the main floor, they even gave him a small drink allotment.

It was on the main floor that I noticed just how much James was peeing. It was also when I noticed just how big my belly was getting. All of the sodium they were giving James was making him pee like crazy. He would soak right through his Pull-Ups, and the first day we were on the main floor, I changed his bedding eight times. In the PICU, the nurse is constantly there, helping. It's harder to get the nurse's attention out on the main floor, and I've never been good about asking for help. But when Jon called that night, I was exhausted. I had puffy, thirty-five-week-pregnant ankles, not the slim, eighteen-week ankles I should have had. My belly muscles were tight and sore, as was my back. My mom had been planning to come to help us when we got home from the hospital, but I told my husband I needed her there now. He agreed, and at about 10:00 at night, I called my mom in Michigan and asked her to come. She was there thirty-six hours later.

And it was a good thing she came. James was on the main floor of the hospital only two days. During that time, his sodium dropped back down to below 120, and by the time my mom arrived, he was back in the PICU.

Once back in the PICU, the doctors began the exact same treatment they had done only a few days before to get his sodium up in the high 120s. I kept wondering and kept asking about the long-term plan. Clearly James couldn't stay hooked up to a super-concentrated IV solution the rest of his life. No one had any answers.

I couldn't sleep in James's room as long as he was in the PICU, so my mom and I were staying at the hotel down the street from the hospital. One morning, as we were walking the short, half-block distance from the hotel to the hospital, I started to complain about the financial cost Jon and I would incur over the next few months as the medical bills would start to pour in, not to mention the hotel cost, parking, eating out, etc. It seemed like almost all of James's life we had been tied down with various medical or therapy bills from all of James's health issues. But this past year had been very uneventful, so as some of our funds started to free up, we had begun to dream big. And as a result, Jon and I had been diligently saving over the past six months so that we could initiate a big ministry idea that we had. My mom knew all our plans, and as the sidewalk between the hotel and hospital passed by under my feet, I unrolled all of my disappointments and frustrations about how we weren't going to hit our saving goals now. I wondered why God was taking this opportunity from us. It wasn't like we were saving for a lake house.

As we stopped to wait at the intersection directly in front of the hospital, I had run out of complaints.

My mom didn't say much. After a brief pause, she simply said, "I guess it will just have to happen some other way."

No more needed to be said as we crossed the street into the hospital. *Patience*, I thought. *God's way, not our way.*

It took several more days, but James's sodium did return to the high 120s, and this time they took him off the IV and put him on an oral sodium supplement while continuing to restrict his fluid intake. After monitoring him for a few days in the PICU, his levels remained in the mid-to-high 120s, so they decided again to send him out to the main floor. It was another two days of monitoring out there when they finally said we could go home.

He wasn't discharged until later that evening, but the same morning of his discharge, I had to return to Greensboro for the big anatomy ultrasound for our babies. This was the same type of ultrasound that we had for James when we found out there was something wrong with his head. We had already had a quick look at the babies' heads earlier, and everything looked okay. Still, I was anxious to get the official word.

I had been sending prayer request e-mails and updates about James to many of my friends and family throughout our hospital stay, and that day, when I returned to the hospital, I was happy to report that both babies looked healthy in every way. I wrote this as an update:

> As I left Duke early this morning and drove back to Greensboro for my ultrasound, I had some time to think in the car by myself and listen to some good music that described Jesus and all of His great attributes. You know I don't often react too negatively to bad news, and I tend to not get too excited about good news either. I know people don't often understand this (and I'm not an emotional person in general), but as I was driving, it occurred to me that Jesus Christ is my light; He is my strength; He is my sure foundation, my greatest joy, my deepest love, my truest pleasure; and He is always the same, no matter what is happening in my life. So great is the joy of knowing Him that even the good news that this life offers us can sometimes seem like lighting a small candle outside on a bright sunny day. The small light is no comparison to the big light. But still I thank Him for this great news today about all my precious babies, but mostly I thank Him for choosing me to have a relationship with Him and for loving me unconditionally.

James would have to remain on the oral sodium supplement after leaving the hospital—which tasted like drinking ocean water, as far as I could tell—four times a day. He also had to continue his fluid restriction of only a half liter per day. Altogether, we went home after seventeen days with a complicated medication regiment that required fourteen different syringes of medicine per day.

It wasn't until our follow-up appointment with the mustached nephrologist that it fully sank in for me that this might be a permanent condition. I was anxious to get James off some of those medications and hopefully allow him to drink just a bit more. He was getting so mad at me when his little allotment was finished and I wouldn't let him have any more to drink. But at the nephrologist appointment, James's sodium was only 124, so the mustached doctor recommended no changes.

I was exhausted and uncomfortable being pregnant with twins, so I was glad there were still almost two weeks left of school before the summer break. I had arranged for James's teacher to give him one of his sodium supplements at school, and after a few days of being home, James was back on the bus.

There were about four days left before the end of the school year when James's teacher called just as I was waking up from my nap. "James doesn't seem to be doing very good today. He's very lethargic, and we can't get him to participate in any of our classroom activities. He's just not himself," she said.

"Are his arms and legs cold to the touch?" I asked, thinking back to those first few days in the hospital when I was so worried about losing him.

She had to go check and call me back. When I picked up the phone, she sounded even more concerned. "Yes, his arms and legs are very cold. He's so lethargic we just can't get him to do anything."

I sat there in silence on the phone until it became just too awkward and I was forced to say something. "I don't know what to do," I said. "I'm going to come get him, but it might take me longer because I'm going to call the doctor first and ask him what I should do."

Thankfully, there is always a doctor on-call at Duke for each of the disciplines, so I put in a call-me-back request and began packing my bags. Again, my mind wandered back to the day I packed for only a two-night stay in the hospital only to end up being there for seventeen days.

Will we end up there again? I thought.

I decided to pack enough clean clothes for another two-day stay.

I was actually scheduled to teach a Bible study that afternoon.

Maybe James will be fine and he can come with me to the study, I thought.

So I packed two bags—one for the hospital and one for my study—grabbed my cell phone, and was headed out the door when the phone rang.

It was the pediatric nephrologist on-call. I explained to him that my son was acting very similar to the way he was acting when his sodium was down at 106.

"So what do you want me to do?" he asked.

I couldn't help but let out a short chuckle. I was calling him so he could tell *me* what to do. But I knew he was right. I knew what my options were and the consequences of each decision. There were no clear answers. It was completely up to me.

"Well," I said, "yesterday I had his blood drawn at a local lab here, and I haven't heard about the results. If I give you their number, do you think you could track that down? As a doctor, you might have more success than me."

James had been poked so much that I hated to take him to have it done again. The doctor agreed, and by the time I reached the school parking lot, he had phoned back.

"His sodium level yesterday was one twenty-nine," he said.

I was so relieved.

His teacher was also relieved, and we both concluded that maybe he was just tired. As I packed James up in the car to head for my Bible study, I prayed, *Well, Lord. I guess this is just the way it's going to be for the rest of my life. You sure have a way of keeping me on my knees! Once again, I'm here in this place where my options are to go crazy with worry or to put my trust completely in You.*

I glanced back at James, strapped in his car seat. "I love you, James," I said.

"I wove you too, Mom," he said.

I smiled, remembering the time when I wondered if he would ever be able to speak those words to me.

I paused, certain that I didn't want to be in this position again but knowing that choosing crazy with worry was not a good option. I began reflecting over the past six years, at how God had taken care of us so many times when it seemed like all hope was gone. Somewhere deep down inside, I knew that one of these days it might not all work out the way I imagine good to be. But I thought back to that e-mail I had written. Did I really mean it? Was God really bigger and better than both any good news or bad? I didn't hesitate at all. He *was*. And after all these years, through all these trials, I knew it now more surely than I knew anything I could see or touch or feel. And by the time I reached my study, I was able to once again put the life of my precious little boy completely in the hands of my Savior.

Now when Jesus came into the district of Caesarea Philippi, He was asking His disciples, "Who do people say that the Son of Man is?" And they said, "Some say John the Baptist; and others, Elijah; but still others, Jeremiah, or one of the prophets." He said to them, "But who do *you* say that I am?" Simon Peter answered, "You are the Christ, the Son of the living God."

Matthew 16:13-16 (emphasis mine)

Sometimes God sees us put forth some initiative. Or perhaps we pray and tell God that we will choose to make ourselves available for His service. Or maybe we take advantage of an opportunity to serve that fits hand-in-glove with our spiritual gifts and talents, and we really feel like God is using us or will continue to use us for some great kingdom-building thing. Then before we get too far down that path, we get hit with a terrible trial, and all the things that we thought were so great and well intentioned get completely derailed.

A similar thing happened to Moses in the Old Testament. Acts 7:22 tells us how, growing up in Pharaoh's household, he became "educated in all the learning of the Egyptians, and he was a man of power in words and deeds." It sounds as if he had built many skills and abilities, and as he approached the age of forty, he couldn't help but think that he might be the one to put all these great skills and power to use to free his people.

> It entered his mind to visit his brethren, the sons of Israel. And when he saw one of them being treated unjustly, he defended him and took vengeance for the oppressed by striking down the Egyptian. And he supposed that his brethren understood that God was granting them deliverance through him, but they did not understand.
>
> Acts 7:23b-25

Moses had a plan. It seemed to him to be a godly plan. He wasn't going to sit around and waste his life in the palace. He would risk his power and position to help God's people. He tried to stand up and be their leader, but they rejected him, saying, "Who made you a ruler and judge over us?" (Acts 7:27)

And so Moses was run out of town. He had a plan, a dream to be used by God. But God's answer was, "No," or at least, "Not now." So for forty years, Moses lived out in the desert. And by the time God finally did come to him, saying He would use Moses to deliver His people, Moses's response was quite different than the first time. He said, "Who am I, that I should go to Pharaoh, and that I should bring the sons of Israel out of Egypt?" (Exodus 3:11). Then the Lord sent him off with great signs and wonders at his disposal, and standing on the banks of the Red Sea, Moses was able to say, "Stand by and see the salvation of the LORD which He will accomplish for you today..." (Exodus 14:13b).

As we've learned from His Word, God is in control. Not only is He in control of our trials, but He is in control of the great opportunities we have in life. And sometimes, by His grace, He chooses to use us to further His kingdom. But even these opportunities are completely within His control. And even if that opportunity never comes, it doesn't necessarily mean that God is not pleased with you.

After Moses had led the people safely out of Egypt, God commanded him to go enter the land that He promised to Abraham. But Moses had learned that he could not do anything like that on his own. He replied to God, "If Your presence does not go with us, do not lead us up from here" (Exodus 33:15). He learned that while he had some skills and abilities on his own, if God was not behind it, he'd better not even try it.

My husband and I still dream of a great ministry opportunity. And we continue to make plans for some specific things. But right now it seems clear that we just have to wait. God knows our hearts, and I hope that when the time is right and when we are transformed into what He wants us to be, we will be given a great opportunity—one in which He receives all the glory.

Once, Jesus asked His disciples what people were saying about Him. Just like in our day today, some people thought He was a great teacher or even a prophet. But then Jesus made the question much more personal. "Who do you say that I am?" You see, it doesn't matter what others think or say. Someday we will stand before God to give an account. We will not stand there with our spouse or our parent or with our pastor or church. We will stand there alone. There will be no doubt in your mind about your guilt and all the ways you rebelled against God. There will only be the realization of the answer to one significant question: "Who do you say that I am?" Peter's answer was the correct one. He truly believed that Jesus was the Christ, the Messiah, the Holy One, his Creator, the Son of the Living God, God Himself in the flesh.

So I ask you now. Who do *you* say that Jesus is? If He truly is the Almighty God Himself, then there is no reason to not trust Him. There is no reason to not consider it all joy when you encounter various trials. If you find yourself struggling with God about the road He's given you to walk, your struggle is really not about your situation but about what you believe about Jesus. Is He in control, or do you still want that to be you? Can you put your situation completely in His hand and trust Him with it? If He is the God He says He is, there should be no reason not to trust Him completely. Do you believe that God will make it all worth it when you get to heaven like He said He would?

A friend recently sent me a quote: "It's not what you believe; it's what you believe enough to do."

CONCLUSION

There is a common theme throughout the Bible concerning trials: perseverance. Perseverance is more than just getting by. It means making a continued effort to achieve something of value despite the difficulties, sorrow, or opposition. Rather than just letting life happen to you, when you persevere, you move steadily toward a goal. My goals for James are that someday he will walk on his own and be able to go hiking with his brother and sister. I want him to have a job that requires a skill so that he can become a contributing member of society. And I want to teach him the Bible so that he will understand enough to be able to choose to accept Jesus Christ as his God and Savior. But we must hold our goals with an open hand. We cannot expect that God will always give us exactly what we reach for. But that doesn't mean that we can't live in great anticipation that He will do something God-sized in our life.

I've walked through over seventeen thousand five hundred and twenty hours with James since he was released from the hospital after his sixth birthday. Sure, it would be easier to just say it's been over two years. But we don't live life in big chunks like that. We live, and often struggle, though life one hour at a time. And each new hour, we have to choose again to trust God with the specific situation He has given us. So be encouraged by God's Word, anticipate that God is building something of great value in your life's circumstance; hope big, choose joy, serve the Lord with gladness, and make the best choices you can make in *this* hour. Let the love of Christ control you so that you no longer live for yourself but for Him, who died and rose again on your behalf (2 Corinthians 5:13-15).

ENDNOTES

I Am Fearfully and Wonderfully Made

1 Francis A. Schaeffer, *Escape from Reason* (Downers Grove, IL: InterVarsity Press, 1968), 21.

2 Ravi Zacharias, "Jesus Among Other Gods," RZIM (Norcross, GA), 2007.

3 Schaeffer, 24.

4 David A. DeWitt, *Answering the Tough Ones* (Grand Rapids, MI: Relational Concepts, Inc., 1993), 75-84.

5 James Strong, *The New Strong's Expanded Exhaustive Concordance of the Bible* (Nashville, TN: Thomas Nelson, 2010), #3986.

6 David A. DeWitt, "The Book of James: A Commentary" (Grand Rapids, MI: Relational Concepts, 1999), 3.

7 *Footprints*, author unknown.

The Lord Has Made Everything for Its Own Purpose

8 Lois Flowers, *Infertility: Finding God's Peace in the Journey* (Harvest House Publishers, 2003), 19.

Do Not Regard Lightly the Discipline of the Lord

9   Watchman Nee, *The Breaking of the Outer Man and the Release of the Spirit* (Anaheim, CA: Living Stream Ministry), 68.

10 Don Miller, "Beautifully Broken: The Self-Life," Westover Church (Greensboro, NC), August 23, 2009.

11 Nee, 98.

12 Strong, #3809.

If I Want Him to Remain, What Is That to You?

13 Nee, 80.

14 Flowers, 66.

Desire Realized Is Sweet to the Soul

15 John Eldredge, *The Journey of Desire: Searching for the Life We've Only Dreamed Of* (Thomas Nelson: Nashville, TN, 2000), 36.

Consider It All Joy When You Encounter Various Trials

16 Strong, #5479.

17 *Webster's Ninth New Collegiate Dictionary* (Springfield, MA: Merriam-Webster, 1990), 652.

18   Strong, #3956.

19   Strong, #3986.

20   Strong, #2233.

21   Nee, 39-40.

I Go to Prepare a Place for You

22   Don & Susie Van Ryn and Newell, Colleen & Whitney
      Cerak, *Mistaken Identity: Two Families, One Survivor,
      Unwavering Hope* (New York: Howard Books, 2008),
      143-144.

23   Richard Wurmbrand, "The Christian Revolution," *The
      Voice of the Martyrs*, March 2007, 11.

Momentary Light Affliction

24   Nee, 13.

25   Nee, 15.